140 SPECIES IN FULL COLOR

ENDANGERED ANIMALS

a Golden Guide® from St. Martin's Press

by
GEORGE S. FICHTER

Illustrated by
KRISTIN KEST

St. Martin's Press ❧ **New York**

FOREWORD

The challenge of this book was indeed great: to make it clear that on our present course we are headed toward ecological catastrophe, toward a time when hundreds of species, large and small, will literally become extinct every day and when even humanity will be threatened.

Although many extinctions are inevitable, not all is gloom and doom. There have been some truly remarkable turn-arounds in which endangered species have, usually with our help, made a comeback. Past errors are extremely difficult to correct, but some amends are being made, and fewer travesties are being committed today. With the growing awareness worldwide that the earth is fragile and that all of its creatures are interdependent, there is certainly hope for the future.

Thanks are due the artist, Kristin Kest, for depicting these animals. Thanks are due also to Maury Solomon, Caroline Greenberg, and Henry Flesh for engineering and editing this book, and to Nadine, my wife, for her continued understanding and tolerance.

G.S.F.

CONTENTS

Tyrannosaurus Rex
roaming the swamps of
the late Cretaceous period

INTRODUCTION

ENDANGERMENT is not a new phenomenon. Along with extinctions, it has been going on for as long as there has been life on earth. Scientists estimate that for every species alive today, at least a hundred others that once existed became endangered and are now extinct, gone forever. Looked at another way, 99 percent of all species that have ever existed on earth are no longer here.

The dinosaurs are the classic example of an entire group of animals that became extinct. For more than 167 million years, they were the dominant creatures on earth. Some of the hundreds of species were no larger than chickens. Others were fearsome beasts of tremendous size. The largest of these measured more than 100 feet long, from snout to tip of tail, and weighed more than 50 tons. Some species stood 20 feet tall and walked on their hind legs.

During the heyday of the dinosaurs, the earth was warm, even in the polar regions. Then, about 65 million years ago, the dinosaurs mysteriously died out. Some scientists attribute this to a general drop in temperature, perhaps caused by a catastrophic collision of the earth with an asteroid. The once warm, swampy lowlands became cool and dry. For the giant reptiles (and more than two thirds of the existing marine life) the earth became a hostile environment. Taking the dinosaurs' place were warm-blooded creatures more suited to living in the cooler environment—mammals.

The earth has undergone many changes over the millennia. There have been periods of extensive mountain building and intense volcanic activity. There have been great and small ice ages, with glaciers advancing and then retreating. The earth has been struck by meteorites and comets, and the sun's solar output has varied over time. Each time a great change has taken place on earth, plants and animals not suited for survival in the altered environment have died out and been replaced by others.

MASS EXTINCTIONS have occurred at least five times over the last half-billion years, including the episode that ended the reign of the dinosaurs. During these five episodes, huge numbers of species were suddenly annihilated. In addition to mass extinctions, many species have died out slowly over the millennia, due mostly to the winnowing processes of natural selection and survival of the fittest.

Each time a mass extinction has occurred, the earth has recovered completely from it. In fact, there are more species alive today than ever before in the earth's history—perhaps as many as 100 million.

Many scientists believe that the earth is currently experiencing yet another episode of mass extinctions. But the extinctions today are being caused by humans rather than by "natural" events. In addition, most extinctions today are occurring at rapidly accelerated rates. Even the so-called sudden mass extinctions of the past took place over many thousands of years. Extinctions today can be measured in terms of a human lifetime. For example, since the discovery of North America by the Europeans in the late 1400s, more than 60 species of North American vertebrates have become extinct, nearly all within the last 100 years. At least 10 percent of all the animals with backbones in the United States are now in danger of becoming extinct.

Some scientists believe that extinctions are taking place worldwide at the rate of at least one species every day, and that this rate may increase. If that is true, then within the next few decades, we may well lose more than a quarter of the earth's total number of species.

Why be concerned about this? After all, the earth has recovered from earlier mass extinctions. But these recoveries took many millions of years. And with the kinds of losses we are currently experiencing, a full recovery in any span of time that is meaningful to humanity is highly unlikely.

The endangered Hawksbill Turtle. Many sea turtles are facing extinction today, threatening the biodiversity of the seas.

BIODIVERSITY is the term used by scientists to refer to the vast variety of living species on earth whose combined functioning keeps the earth's natural cycles, such as the water and nitrogen cycles, running smoothly. Creatures not yet even named by scientists help serve important ecological functions, such as waste decomposition or the regeneration of oxygen into the atmosphere. The loss of just a few species in an ecosystem can cause that entire ecosystem to collapse.

ENERGY must also be continually transferred among specific groups of plants and animals in an ecosystem. The various species form the food chains, food pyramids, and other intricate relationships that tie all the different forms of life on earth together. A simple food chain has only three steps—from the plants (the producers), to plant-eating consumers (the herbivores), to meat-eating consumers (the carnivores). With death and decay, organic matter is recycled into the system.

FOOD WEBS are made up of food chains, which are interwoven with other food chains, thus forming complex food webs. A break in any part of a food chain affects many others in a food web. Food pyramids are often used to show the relative quantities of living matter, or biomass, in each segment of the food chain. The base of a pyramid represents the producers—the many plants needed to support the few predators, or carnivores, at the top. Many animals that occupy the top of food pyramids today are endangered. This is a clear signal of trouble at the bottom.

Every plant and animal shares in putting together the whole picture of life on earth. No species can be destroyed without it affecting other species, which affects still other species, and so on. And whatever is threatening other species may well also be a threat to human life.

In addition, each species is a unique product of evolution. Each has certain abilities and adaptations that make it special. When any species disappears, its particular combination of genes is lost, and something truly unique is gone forever. Gene "pools," developed over millions of years, are irretrievably lost, thus threatening the earth's biodiversity.

One example can show how biodiversity helps to maintain the balance in nature. The Dodo (see p. 113), which ate the fruit of the Dodo Tree, became extinct in 1680. The trees continued to grow and produce fruit after the birds were gone, but no seeds sprouted. The species appeared to be headed for extinction. Then, in the 1970s, with only 13 trees still remaining, a scientist guessed the problem. When they had passed through the Dodo's gizzard, the seeds' hard outer coats had broken, releasing the embryo plants inside. The scientist fed the fruit to turkeys, which are about the size the Dodoes had been, and the turkeys processed the seeds as the Dodoes had. Thus, the Dodo Tree was saved. But many relationships in an ecosystem are much more complex and are difficult to put back in order.

ADVANCING HUMAN CIVILIZATION has been a chief factor in modern extinctions. As the human population continues to grow, it uses an increasingly large proportion of the earth's resources. Also, throughout their history, people have striven to change the world to make it a more livable place for themselves, often disregarding the needs of the creatures with whom they share this planet. There are many destructive effects of such trends, including habitat loss, pollution, and threats to native species by introduced animals. Hunting, in some cases, also adds to the problem.

HABITAT LOSS is the greatest threat to wildlife today. It happens mainly when land, especially tropical land, is cleared for farming, for the grazing of livestock, or for living space. In South America, for example, the tropical forests are disappearing at a rate of 27,000 square miles every year. This is the habitat for an estimated 50 percent of all land-dwelling plant and animal species. We may never know many of these species, some of which might have proven to be valuable sources of food or medicine.

The clearing of the biologically rich rainforest in northwestern Brazil proceeds at a steady pace even today.

POLLUTION of the natural world with billions of tons of toxic chemicals and with plastics and other wastes that are not biodegradable is a major threat today. Fertilizers, combined with the use of pesticides and herbicides, have certainly helped to increase current food supplies and improve human health, but the long-term effects can be devastating.

INTRODUCTIONS OF SPECIES to new environments may threaten native species by robbing them of food or living space or by spreading new diseases. Alternatively, native species may be preyed upon by introduced species. Island species are particularly vulnerable to such invasions.

HUNTING for the sport of killing or to harvest meat or hides can also be harmful. Often the strongest animals are killed, leaving only the weak to reproduce. Some kills are made only to supply fashion or curio markets. Controlled hunting may sometimes be justified to keep a population healthy.

The bearlike Hairy-nosed Wombat of Australia, a marsupial, was hunted to near extinction for its pelt.

THE ENDANGERED SPECIES ACT (ESA), passed by the United States in 1973, is the most powerful law of its kind in the world. Endangered species are defined as ones that are currently in danger of becoming extinct. Threatened (or "rare") species are not in immediate danger but may become endangered soon. All demand our attention.

Grevy's Zebra is one of several zebras on the endangered species list.

Administered by the federal Fish and Wildlife Service, the ESA considers illegal any activity that reduces the survival chances of an endangered species. It recognizes that all living things are important, not just the big or the beautiful or those valued for sport or commercial reasons. The ESA currently protects some 700 plant and animal species; about 4,000 more are candidates for formal listing.

Opponents of the ESA think it is too wide-ranging and protects even "insignificant" species. They want the law repealed or weakened. Proponents insist that no one species is insignificant, that all serve some purpose in the grand scheme of life on earth, even if we do not yet recognize that purpose.

The ESA, which has served as a model for similar laws elsewhere, may be modified in the future. But it has already had great impact. It has focused attention on the world wildlife crisis and demonstrated that extinction need not be inevitable.

NATIONAL PARKS AND SANCTUARIES have also helped some groups of endangered animals. In many of these places, people can observe and appreciate wildlife while reestablishing their own ties with nature and other living creatures. Exposure of people to the wonders of nature has brought about some much-needed understanding and concern for the plight of wildlife. However, the most important function of these lands is to provide habitat sanctuaries for the wildlife of the region. Some areas are off-limits to tourists, for even those with good intentions can be a major threat to some kinds of wildlife, particularly during the breeding season.

MODERN ZOOS have come to represent a last chance on earth for some species. Unlike zoos of the past, which were miserable prisons for short-lived captives, modern zoos seek to provide animals with all the essentials of their original habitat. Zoo animals are well fed and kept in good health while being carefully studied by scientists. In most zoos, in fact, animals live much longer than they would in the wild.

Zoos have also become important breeding grounds for endangered animals. Once dependent on a constant supply of new animals from the wild to replace those lost due to disease or poor living conditions, many zoos are now the *suppliers* of animals to the wild. However, releases can occur only when suitable habitats are available.

The saving of endangered species, through zoos or other endangered-species programs, is not free from controversy. Few would dispute the need to protect species, but the best way to go about it is often subject to debate. With our limited resources, how are we to decide which animals are the most important to save? Who should make those decisions? Should we continue breeding programs where the populations are so low that many animals are seriously inbred? Are we creating weak species lines as a result?

What kinds of animal-release programs are most effective? Should endangered animals bred in captivity be released into the wild, where they might be killed? Should the ESA protect subspecies or hybrids (animals of mixed lineage)? Should a habitat be protected to save a species, even if it means large numbers of people, such as the loggers who cut timber in the endangered Spotted Owl's domain (see p. 62), are put out of work? These and many other questions will need to be seriously addressed in the future as zoos and various other organizations expand their role as the saviors of threatened species.

PEREGRINE FALCONS, which once flew over most of North America, became victims of DDT poisoning. The pesticide, acquired from their prey, caused them to lay weak-shelled eggs that broke before the baby birds could hatch. Less than a quarter of a century after the introduction of DDT in 1946, the Peregrine Falcon seemed doomed to extinction. Since the banning of DDT in the United States in 1972, however, the endangered birds have made a steady comeback. Biologists have helped by removing eggs from nests and hatching the birds in incubators. They later release the young birds when they are fully feathered and capable of living independently. Interestingly, these powerful and swift-flying predators have prospered in cities, where they nest on tall buildings—sometimes in boxes provided for them—and prey on the abundant pigeon populations.

Peregrine Falcon on skyscraper ledge with pigeon prey and brood of young

BIOMES are areas scattered around the earth that contain similar climates and land features and, as a result, harbor similar types of plant and animal life. Grasslands, deserts, mountains, the poles, and temperate and tropical forests are examples of biomes. Biomes provide a natural way of grouping endangered animals. Animals described in this book are generally grouped according to their native biomes. Islands, oceans, and wetlands, though sometimes not considered biomes, can serve that purpose in this book.

Only a representative sampling of endangered amphibians, reptiles, birds, and mammals are included. Not mentioned at all are the countless fish and invertebrates (animals without backbones) as well as plants, all of which are certainly as important in the intricate web of life. Exclusion of them is due only to the particular focus of this

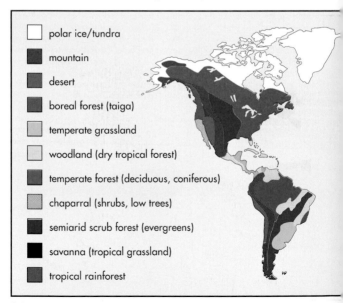

polar ice/tundra

mountain

desert

boreal forest (taiga)

temperate grassland

woodland (dry tropical forest)

temperate forest (deciduous, coniferous)

chaparral (shrubs, low trees)

semiarid scrub forest (evergreens)

savanna (tropical grassland)

tropical rainforest

book and its intent to show how endangerment threatens to drastically alter the world in ways obvious even to us, from our limited human perspective.

Up to 20 percent of all land plants may vanish within the next fifty years. Because plants are the major food source for most living things, as many as ten animal species could disappear for each plant species that becomes extinct. The only survivors may be the many so-called weeds among plants and such hardy and nonspecialized animals as cockroaches, rats, gulls, and other scavenging omnivores. Many animals have already become extinct in modern times. Some of their stories are told here because they remind us of our part in the process. Also included are some remarkable comeback stories, proving that success is possible when serious attention is given to our companions on earth.

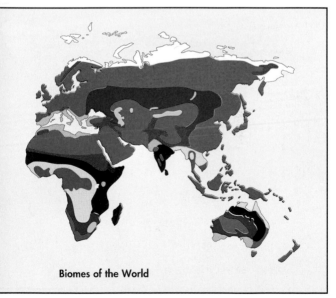

Biomes of the World

GRASSLANDS

Vast seas of grasses once rippled in the wind in the middle of every continent. They were cropped by great herds of grazing animals that inhabited these lands separating the dry deserts from the forests. Along with the grazing animals were the flesh eaters, or carnivores, that preyed on them, scavengers that finished off the remains, and hordes of smaller, burrowing animals that filled every niche in this world of grass.

In temperate regions today, the grasslands are mostly gone, having been converted into fields of grain that are harvested as food for people and their livestock. Grasses still grow on the open lands of the tropics and subtropics, but there the cinch also draws tighter for wildlife as people cultivate these lands to satisfy their own needs.

The heartland of North America was originally a huge prairie—the Great Plains. From the evergreen forests of Canada to the deserts of Mexico and from the Rockies eastward almost to the Mississippi, a waving green sea of grass grew on the flat or gently rolling land. On the eastern side, close to the Mississippi River and its tributaries, the grass grew as high as 10 feet. Toward the drier eastern slopes of the Rockies, the grass was shorter and tougher. These lands were host to herds of some 55 million American Bison and an estimated 35 million Pronghorns. Smaller animals in uncountable numbers shared the grasslands with them.

No land area on earth has supported a greater variety of big animals than the African savanna. About 600 miles wide, it borders on Africa's wet and dry tropical forests. To the north and south are deserts. Near the tropical forests the grasses are thick and tall, and scattered across the flat land

The Serengeti Plains in Africa are among the richest grasslands in the world.

17

are scrubby trees. Nearer the desert regions, the grasses are short, and the land is treeless or has only a sprinkling of thorny shrubs. The savanna originally occupied about 4 million square miles, or nearly 40 percent of the great African continent.

Today the savanna is home to about 40 species of large animals. Millions of these animals once inhabited the savanna, but since the arrival of the Europeans some 300 years ago, their habitat has shrunk year by year and their populations have decreased greatly.

Wildlife is threatened throughout southeastern Asia, too, which is populated by roughly 600 million people. A few large animals, including some leopards and tigers, have managed to survive, but everywhere wildlife is endangered due to hunting and the destruction of habitats.

Long under cultivation, the Eurasian steppes to the north support only scattered populations of wild creatures today. This grassland area, scorched by intense heat in summer and then frozen in winter, is nevertheless heavily populated by people.

Nearly 40 percent of Australia's land is essentially grassland. Here can be found most of Australia's unusual animals, many of which are endangered today.

The heartland of South America consists of the *pampas,* a treeless plain that in most South American countries has been converted into land for grazing livestock or growing crops. In Brazil the grasslands are called the *campos;* in Colombia and Venezuela, the *llanos.* Only the most hostile of these lands have been left to wildlife—lands where the temperature is too high, there is little rain, or the winds blow too strongly to suit the needs of people and their livestock. Here many wild creatures escape the ravages of nature by living in burrows most of the time or migrating to more temperate climates when conditions become unbearable.

QUAGGAS were zebras that once lived on the African savanna. Their name came from the sounds they made, which some people thought resembled the barking of a dog. Unlike the markings of other zebras, a Quagga's stripes were confined to the front of its body; the rear half of its body was a uniform yellowish brown.

Although the Quagga was never as abundant as other grazers, it nevertheless roamed the savanna in large herds of many thousands.

European settlers hunted Quaggas both for their flesh and their hides, which were made into shoes, bags, and other items.

As in many other such cases, the killings were more like massacres than hunts. As early as 1800, the Quagga had begun to be scarce, and the last of the animals in the wild fell before a gun in 1879. A female lived in the Amsterdam Zoo until 1883; then she died without leaving any offspring, as had all the others kept in captivity.

Quagga

19

OSTRICHES now live in the wild only on the grasslands of Africa, although they once roamed over similar lands in Syria and Arabia. These largest of all living birds may stand 8 feet tall and weigh 350 pounds. They have two toes on each foot and can run up to 40 miles per hour, fast enough to outdistance most pursuers. If cornered, they slash with the claws on the ends of their toes, making them formidable foes even to large animals. But their defenses have not protected them from the encroachment of civilization and hunters who are after their skin, meat, eggs, and graceful tail plumes, which are used for decoration.

RHEAS are 5½-feet-tall flightless birds that roam the pampas of South America in flocks of 20 to 30. There are two species. In both, a cock makes a nest in which a harem of three to seven hens lay their eggs—totaling 30 or more. The cock incubates the eggs. Although the newly hatched chicks can run immediately, the cock continues to care for them for several months. Like the Ostriches of Africa and the Emus of Australia, rheas could often be seen peacefully grazing with cattle in times past. But larger herds of livestock and hunting have lately made rheas far more scarce.

EMUS are big flightless birds, the Australian counterparts of the Ostrich of Africa and the rheas of South America. Once there were three species. Now only one exists, and it is rapidly becoming rare.

An Emu stands about 6 feet tall and weighs about 100 pounds. It has a broad, flat, ducklike bill. It can run faster than 30 miles per hour and usually travels in small flocks.

Emus have been hunted as food, and their eggs were once collected and eaten. Because they often compete with livestock for food and also help themselves to wheat crops, Emus were once targeted for killing by the Australian government. However, the birds are now protected by law.

Ostrich

Darwin's Rhea

Emu

21

Lesser Prairie Chicken

LESSER PRAIRIE CHICKENS are one of several chickenlike, or gallinaceous, birds that existed in large numbers on the Great Plains of North America. When the prairies were fenced, these free-roaming birds were forced into small remnants of their once-spacious habitat. They were also heavily hunted, often strictly for sport—the dead birds left lying where they fell. Both the Greater Prairie Chicken and the slightly smaller Lesser Prairie Chicken are seriously declining and can be saved from extinction only by giving them sanctuary on large tracts of protected grassland. There the cocks can once again boom and strut for their mates in early spring, and hens can shepherd their chicks in safety.

WHOOPING CRANES are among the rarest birds in North America. The remaining 250 or so—the total increasing slightly every year since the 1960s—summer in Canada and winter along the Gulf Coast in Texas. Though they are making a comeback, the population is still very vulnerable and could be totally eliminated by a single natural disaster, such as a hurricane or rampant disease.

The Whooping Crane, at more than 4 feet tall the tallest bird in North America, was never abundant. There may never have been more than 1,500 individuals even at the bird's population peak. But Whooping Cranes were originally widely distributed, with their greatest concentration in the Great Plains region. Encroachment by civilization was one of the major reasons for their decline. Overhunting and conversion of the prairie wetlands to farms added to the problem. Today, collisions of fledglings with power lines are the main cause of death. But conservationists and concerned citizens in both Canada and the United States have rallied to the bird's protection. No one ever expects the Whooping Crane, with its 6-foot wingspan, to become abundant or even to reach its original population. But it appears to have at least temporarily been spared total annihilation.

Whooping Crane

KANGAROOS, marsupial mammals strongly identified with Australia, are mostly victims of habitat destruction. The degradation of grasslands by domestic livestock and introduced rabbits have rendered the habitats of many smaller, grass-dwelling species useless. Also, the introduction of predators such as the European Red Fox, dogs, and cats has cut down on the numbers of some species. Finally, some kangaroos are shot as pests or for their pelts. Protective laws are helping, but for some species, the laws may be too late.

The roughly 50 kangaroo species range from rat-size to kangaroos that stand more than 6 feet tall. Nearly two dozen of these species are now endangered.

Both the Red and Eastern Gray Kangaroo are the giants of the group, measuring 6 to 8 feet long from nose to tip of tail. In constant conflict with ranchers, they are now threatened. Swift runners, they often make the fatal mistake of stopping to look back when pursued. At that instant they become easy marks for hunters.

Also endangered is the Short-nosed Rat Kangaroo, the last of four closely related species that once lived all over the continent. The Rat Kangaroo does best on the offshore islands, where it doesn't have to compete with more aggressive foragers such as introduced rabbits. The Rat Kangaroo has also been a victim of habitat destruction and extermination programs designed to get rid of vermin.

Hare Wallabies were once quite common on the grasslands of western Australia but are now extremely rare. Also members of the kangaroo family, they have the amazing ability to jump to a height of 8 feet or more. Along with several other species of wallabies, they were unable to compete successfully with domestic livestock. Some were also exterminated by vermin-control programs. Several species of rock wallabies that inhabit Australia's rocky, hilly country have fared better because they do not have to compete with livestock and rabbits.

Red Kangaroo

**Eastern Gray
Kangaroo**

**Short-nosed
Rat Kangaroo**

Hare Wallaby

25

Morro Bay Kangaroo Rat

MORRO BAY KANGAROO RATS measure about 12 inches long, half of this length consisting of their tail. With their long hind legs, these rodents look very much like miniature kangaroos, and they also hop like them. They feed at night on seeds, nuts, and leaves, carrying any excess booty back to their nest. About two dozen species live in the American Southwest and northern Mexico. Of these, the Morro Bay Kangaroo Rat of California is in the greatest danger of being driven out of existence by encroaching civilization. Both state and federal governments now protect it.

BLACK-TAILED PRAIRIE DOGS were once the most abundant animals on the Great Plains, their total population in the hundreds of millions. Prairie dog "towns" dotted the grasslands. Each consisted of a thousand or more animals, but one huge "city" is estimated to have covered more than 30,000 square miles.

Despite these large numbers, prairie dog populations were kept in check. Each family marked off an area to accommodate its needs. If a trespasser from another group entered a family's territory, it was promptly whistled at until it scurried back to its own family. But venturing more than a hundred feet from the entrance to a burrow was dangerous, for in the grass "jungle" there were coyotes and other predators. When the bison herds came and trampled down the grass, the prairie dogs could spot predators more easily. If there was any sign of danger, a prairie dog would give a shrill alarm "whistle" that would send all of the animals diving into their burrows. Predators such as badgers and the Black-footed Ferret often followed them into their burrows, but this was part of the natural scheme.

Settlers became the greatest threat. The burrows were a menace to horses, which could easily break a leg by stepping into one of the holes. Farmers plowing the prairie land did not like the mounds and holes or the hordes of little rodents eating their field and vegetable crops. Shot, poisoned, or simply driven away, the Black-tailed Prairie Dog just about disappeared, like the bison. The magnitude of the event was less noticeable only because of the longer time involved and the smaller size (about 12 inches) of the animals. Once unbelievably plentiful, they now exist in greatly diminished numbers, as do some of the animals that either preyed on them or, like the Burrowing Owl, lived peacefully with them in their burrows.

Black-tailed
Prairie Dogs

BLACK-FOOTED FERRETS became victims of the campaign to eradicate Black-tailed Prairie Dogs, their principal prey. Never abundant and once reported to be extinct, the Black-footed Ferret has been sighted again. It is now protected by law and should increase in number.

PINK FAIRY ARMADILLOS are among the more than 20 species of armadillos that range over most of South and Central America, particularly in the pampas. The Nine-banded Armadillo has even extended its range into the southern United States in recent years. The Pink Fairy Armadillo, found only in the pampas, measures less than 6 inches long; it is the smallest armadillo and also the rarest. This diminutive creature has only a partial shell, which sits on its head and back as though added as an afterthought. It spends most of its life in a burrow. As with other armadillos, its diet is primarily insects, but it will eat almost any small animal it can catch. Farming has robbed this animal of its habitat, and unfortunately it is often treated as a pest, even though—like other armadillos—it does no serious damage.

Black-footed Ferret

Pink Fairy Armadillo

African Wild Dog

AFRICAN WILD DOGS, which are also known as Cape Hunting Dogs, are nearing extinction. Less than 4,000 exist today, primarily as a result of conflicts with humans. Blamed for the depletion of other wildlife and also for preying on livestock, they have been killed both with guns and with poisons. Lately they have become victims of something even more devastating—diseases picked up from domestic dogs. Conservationists have begun a program of vaccinating the wild dogs (and also infected domestic dogs) to protect against such diseases as rabies and distemper. Large tracts of land are also being set aside where the dogs can avoid contact with people and their animals.

An African Wild Dog stands about 30 inches tall at the shoulders and may weigh as much as 60 pounds. Its coat is a nondescript splotching of yellow, black, and white. The dogs hunt in packs that may consist of ten or more individuals, and when in pursuit of a quarry, they may run at speeds of up to 35 miles per hour for several miles. As with wolves, their kills typically improve the population of the species they prey upon because they take mainly the old, weak, and sick.

29

PAMPAS FOXES live on the grasslands of Chile and Argentina and may also appear along the coasts of these countries. Though at present this fox is not endangered, it is also not abundant. In addition to loss of habitat and pursuit by hunters, it has not coped well with the more aggressive Red Fox, introduced from Europe. Compared to other foxes, the small Pampas Fox (its body is only about 2 feet long) is very slow-moving.

MANED WOLVES live on the pampas of South America. These unusual foxes (they are not wolves) have a foxlike head, a distinct black mane that rises when the animal is excited, and a reddish brown coat. On their long, stiltlike legs they stand almost 3 feet tall at the shoulder and are about 3½ feet in length, excluding their bushy tail. They weigh about 50 pounds. The Maned Wolf is a solitary hunter, preferring small vertebrates such as rodents as well as insects and seasonally available fruit. It has never been abundant and is now in danger of becoming extinct.

HYENAS are often killed simply because of their looks or their unattractive habits. Typically they spend their days sleeping in burrows, then come out at night to prowl for food. They are part of nature's cleanup crew after a predator makes a kill and takes the choice parts. With their powerful jaws, hyenas can crush large bones. They are also aggressive, and working in packs, they sometimes drive off large predators before they have really finished their meals. Two species of hyenas are endangered: the Barbary and the Brown. The Barbary Hyena, a subspecies of the wide-ranging Striped Hyena (which is not endangered), lives in or near Morocco. The secretive Brown Hyena lives in southern Africa, where it spends part of its time on the coast feeding on carrion washed in from the sea. It may also wander the dry interior.

Pampas Fox

Maned Wolf

Barbary Hyena

Brown Hyena

31

Cheetah

CHEETAHS, like all top-of-the-food-chain predators, were never abundant, but today they are very few. The long-legged Cheetah is the fastest of all land animals in short-distance runs—attaining speeds as great as 60 miles per hour in less than a minute. It first walks toward its prey, then speeds up to a sprint. The Cheetah, which is 4 feet long (not including its tail) and has a small head, has lost much of its original habitat as well as its food supply. Further, it has been hunted for its handsome spotted pelt.

Only small numbers of Cheetahs are left on the grass-lands of southern and eastern Africa, including those in Serengeti National Park. Still fewer are found in Asia, where the Cheetah earned the name of Hunting Leopard (though it is not a leopard). There young animals were caught and tamed, then taken onto the plains with a hood over their head. When a herd of Blackbucks was sighted, the hood was slipped off and the swift, eager hunters rushed to make their kill. If successful, the cats were usually given a drink of the slain animal's blood as a reward. In the 1930s the Cheetah was listed as extinct in Asia, but a few have been seen since then.

LIONS live in groups called prides and hunt together, with the lioness usually leading the attack and killing the prey. The male, however, eats first. A male lion is up to 9 feet long, including his tail, and stands 3 feet at the shoulders.

Lions once roamed over most of southern Eurasia, but the few hundred alive today are confined to the Gir Forest of India. They were killed for sport and because they were considered to be extremely dangerous. They will indeed kill domestic livestock when hungry. Lions also almost disappeared from Africa, but large parks have now been set aside where they can exist without threat of annihilation.

Asiatic Lions

33

Przewalski's Horse

PRZEWALSKI'S HORSES survive today in zoos and may still exist in the wild in small numbers on the steppes of Asia. Their rarity is believed to be due to their inability to compete with domestic livestock for food and water in the dry grasslands where they live. These small horses stand about 4 feet tall at the shoulders and have erect, brushlike manes. They are believed to resemble the kind of primitive horse that crossed the bridge of land that joined North America and Asia thousands of years ago.

PAMPAS DEER are now so rare that conservationists fear for their survival. With the disappearance of the tall pampas grass in which these South American natives took refuge, and with hunting of the deer still being allowed, their population has dropped so low that recovery may no longer be possible. Introduction of the strongly competitive Red Deer and Axis Deer from Europe has also been a factor, as have anthrax and foot-and-mouth disease, both of which are transmitted to the Pampas Deer by domestic livestock.

Pampas Deer

Giant Sable
Antelope

GIANT SABLE ANTELOPES are among several antelope species that once roamed the grassy African savanna in large numbers. They are now extremely rare. Noted for their exceptionally long horns, which grow to more than 5 feet, they have been sought after and prized by trophy hunters for centuries. They have also been killed for food. These stately creatures are today increasing their numbers on reserves in Africa, and thus they might be spared the fate of the similar Blue Antelope, which was hunted into extinction before 1900.

35

WHITE-TAILED GNUS, also known as Black Wildebeests, were once common in Africa from the Cape to the Transvaal. Standing less than 4 feet tall at the shoulders, the animal's bristly mane and tufts of hair on its nose make it look ferocious—which it can be. However, it is rare for grazers of this type to be combative. Hunted almost to extinction for their meat and hides more than a century ago, White-tailed Gnus are now protected and appear to be increasing again, from a low of a few hundred animals in the late 1800s to perhaps several thousand today.

PRONGHORNS roamed the Great Plains with the bison. Before the arrival of white settlers, the population of this swift grazing animal is estimated to have been nearly 40 million. The Pronghorn ran fast enough—more than 50 miles per hour—to escape the wolf and the coyote, but it could not escape bullets. The settlers also brought with them plows and began putting up fences. Diminished in number by sport and meat hunters, and with wide-open spaces becoming increasingly scarce, the Pronghorns retreated to more remote areas.

Research shows that Pronghorns do not compete directly with cattle for the same grasses; hence the two can graze on the same land. The Pronghorn also does not spread disease to cattle, as was once believed. As a result of these findings, ranchers have begun helping in efforts to bring back the Pronghorn.

For the present the Pronghorn seems safe, its population at about 250,000. It could be threatened, however, by any large-scale changes in its habitat, such as converting the remaining open rangeland into plowed fields or strip-mining the land for coal.

One subspecies, the Sonoran Pronghorn, which lives on the border between Arizona and Mexico, is definitely endangered today. Only about 450 still exist, and there has been no formal agreement between the United States and Mexico on how to manage these animals to insure their continued survival.

Pronghorns

37

AMERICAN BISON, or buffalo, have survived after almost becoming extinct. Once the sprawling grasslands of central North America were home to an estimated 60 million of these shaggy beasts. Some even ranged eastward across the Mississippi River into the Ohio Valley. Great bulls stood more than 6 feet tall at the shoulders and weighed over a ton. In autumn the huge herds moved southward to warmer lands and an abundant supply of food. In spring they traveled northward again as the grass sprouted tender green shoots under the warming sun.

In this treeless and largely arid land, the bison were the mainstay of the Plains Indians, who used their hides to make garments and tepees and their bones, horns, and teeth to make tools, weapons, and ornaments. The dried, pancake-shaped pieces of dung, or "buffalo chips," were burned as a fuel for both cooking and heating. Enough meat was dried to provide food for the tribe until the next herd passed. No part of a killed bison was wasted.

American Bison

The Indians killed only for their needs, and so they did not seriously decrease the size of the herds. It was white hunters who whittled the herds into near oblivion. With their repeating rifles and then with trains to haul away the meat and hides to markets in the East, they soon significantly reduced the bison population. The hunters were extremely wasteful, often taking only parts of a slaughtered animal, such as the hump or the tongue, and leaving the rest to rot. Sometimes, too, the big animals were shot from train windows simply for sport. The killing was endorsed by the government as a way of driving the Indians away and opening the land for white settlers.

By the 1880s the great herds were gone. In 1889 the 600 remaining bison were herded onto a federal reservation, where they were bred and have prospered. Small herds are kept today on several private and government-managed lands. The bison has thus been spared from becoming only a name in the history books.

ELEPHANTS, the largest of all living land animals, are so much a part of our picture of the African and Asian continents that we cannot imagine the world without them. But that is a distinct possibility.

The Asian Elephant has small, triangular ears, a humped back, a single "finger" on the end of its trunk, and relatively small tusks. The bull, or male, stands about 10 feet tall at the shoulder and weighs up to 6 tons. The more swaybacked African Elephant has huge fanlike ears, two "fingers" on the end of its trunk, and large tusks. The bull may stand 11 feet tall at the shoulder and weigh as much as 7 tons. The females of both species are smaller than the bulls.

An elephant's solid ivory tusks are greatly enlarged incisor teeth. Those of a bull African Elephant may measure more than 11 feet long and weigh 250 pounds each. The tusks are used not only for defense but also for digging and lifting. Normally an elephant has only 4 molar teeth—2 above and 2 below. But behind each tooth are replacements ready to grow in when the old teeth wear away. In its lifetime an elephant uses a total of 24 molars—4 replacements for each original. Each molar has a ridged or corrugated top, measures about 12 inches long and 12 inches wide, and weighs about 9 pounds.

Strictly vegetarian, an elephant in the wild consumes more than 500 pounds of fruits, leaves, and branches daily and drinks about 50 gallons of water first drawn into its trunk and then squirted from the trunk into its throat. In both kinds of elephants the trunk may weigh as much as 250 pounds. Essentially a greatly elongated, double-tubed mobile nose, the trunk is controlled by an intricate set of muscles and is powerful enough to lift logs, yet sensitive enough to pick up tiny twigs or to pluck fruit. The trunk is also used to make loud, trumpeting calls or as a snorkel when the animal walks underwater. Elephants have an acute sense of smell but poor vision.

Asian Elephant

African Elephant

Obviously, elephants need large tracts of land on which to forage. Their big size protects them from all natural predators except humans, but they are victims of poaching for their ivory and of habitat destruction. The remaining herds of elephants are small. How long these giant mammals can survive in their now much more limited world is questionable. Their total population today is less than 10 percent of what it was a century ago.

DESERTS

Deserts are lands with an annual rainfall of less than 10 inches. In hot deserts the daytime temperature commonly rises to more than 100° F and may soar to over 150° F in spots. Nights are usually cool. In mid-latitude deserts, the daytime temperature is generally cool and becomes bitter cold at night. If a desert were defined as just a place with low availability of water, then much of the tundra and also the polar regions might be classified as deserts.

Despite seemingly unlivable conditions, many kinds of animals thrive in deserts. When the rains come—generally in downpours—a desert quickly explodes with an amazing variety of colorful flowers. Plants must produce their fruits and seeds in the short time water is available. The remainder of the year they are dormant, or nearly so.

The Sahara, largest of the world's hot deserts, extends across northern Africa from the Atlantic Ocean to the Red Sea. It is an area equal in size to the United States. On the eastern side of the Red Sea, the desert continues through Asia Minor as the Syrian and Saudi Arabian deserts and is connected through northern India to the cool Gobi Desert of Mongolia. Only parts of this massive desert are sand, but in these areas the sand may be piled to depths of several hundred feet. Swept by the wind, the sand lies in crescent-shaped dunes, like giant waves in the sea. In other places the strong winds have scoured the earth clean, leaving only gravel and bare rock.

Two other deserts in southwestern Africa are the Namib and the Kalahari. The Kalahari is noted for its foglike mists. A large part of the southwestern United States and western Mexico are desert regions, too. South American deserts include the Atacamba, along the Pacific coast of Chile, and the Gran Chaco in western Argentina. In addition, most of central and western Australia is a desert, uninhabitable by humans except along its fringes.

American Southwest desert scene. The right side shows the desert in bloom.

43

GILA MONSTERS are poisonous lizards. The only other poisonous lizard in the world is the similar but slightly larger Beaded Lizard. Both are desert dwellers and both, like venomous snakes, produce a potent poison in modified salivary glands. When the lizards bite—their first defense is trying to escape—they clamp down tightly so that the venom flows from the glands in their lower jaw along grooves in their teeth and into the wound.

The Gila Monster is most abundant in the southwestern United States; the Beaded Lizard is confined to Mexico. Gila Monsters are sluggish and not usually very aggressive, but because they are poisonous, people have killed large numbers of them. The Gila Monster is threatened and is now protected by law in Arizona.

Gila Monster

TORTOISES are land-dwelling turtles. Typically they have a high-arched or domed shell. Their front legs are flipperlike and are used for digging; their hind legs are stumpy and broad, like an elephant's. Giant tortoises that lived on the Galápagos Islands millions of years ago weighed more than a ton. Many tortoises are still found on the Galápagos Islands (see pp. 118-19), where they still grow quite large and heavy, though not as large or heavy as their ancestors.

Like all turtles, tortoises are reptiles. They are also vegetarians. They can survive for long periods without drinking water, getting all the moisture they need from the plants on which they feed and possibly also producing some water metabolically. All three species of tortoises inhabiting the United States, commonly called Gopher Tortoises, are either threatened or endangered. They are victims of the pet trade and of habitat destruction and may also have been hunted for food. The Desert Tortoise of the American Southwest was thought to be safe and abundant until the 1980s, when suddenly its population dropped by more than 50 percent as a result of a respiratory disease. This disease might have been introduced by tortoises kept as pets and then set free. Keeping tortoises as pets is no longer permitted, and lands are being set aside as preserves for the Desert Tortoise.

45

KIT FOXES have very large ears, enabling them to pick up even the slightest sound made by their prey, mice or other rodents. Their big ears also serve as radiators to help get rid of excess body heat in the desert. Kit Foxes are active mainly at night, when the desert is coolest. To escape the heat during the day, the Kit Fox digs a burrow in the sand to a depth of up to 5 feet. Smallest of the North American foxes, Kit Foxes are about 3 feet long and stand only a foot tall at the shoulders. Their grayish brown color helps them blend into their surroundings. Their tail is tipped with black.

These shy, speedy little foxes were hunted heavily for their pelts. Many more were killed by poison baits put out by ranchers whose main target was the Coyote. Kit Foxes have been exterminated over much of their range, but in some areas they have escaped persecution and are possibly even making a comeback to former abundance.

Kit Fox

Addax

ADDAXES are African antelopes with a distinctive black tuft of hair on their forehead. Under this tuft is a butterfly-shaped patch of white that extends around each eye. The male's spiraled and ridged horns may be 3 feet long; females have smaller horns. Both use their horns at least partly as weapons of defense. With its broad, flat hooves, an Addax can travel with ease through the sand. Small herds constantly roam the desert in search of the succulent plants that are their source of moisture as well as nutrition.

Although it occupies land of no value either to humans or to their livestock, the Addax is still threatened with extinction. It is not a fast runner, and so hunters in motor vehicles or even on camels can easily overtake it. Large herds have been reduced to a few hundred animals, and the total population is now believed to be fewer than 10,000 individuals.

47

ARABIAN ORYXES are a type of African oryx. Oryxes are antelopes. Arabian Oryxes and the slightly larger Scimitar-horned Oryxes inhabit the desert fringes. Their herds may travel long distances to find enough food for their needs, and although they will drink water when it is available, they can also survive for long periods with their only source of moisture being the succulent plants on which they feed. Both oryxes have become rare as a result of hunting, done nowadays for sport from motor vehicles and often with machine guns. The oryxes have survived, but only because those kept in captivity have not only thrived but also produced young. Captive-bred oryxes have been reintroduced to the countries of Oman and Jordan.

BONTEBOKS, or Moroccan Dorcases, are one of half a dozen African gazelles that are now endangered. Only small herds exist today. Like other open-country species, these long-legged fleet animals are victims of encroaching civilization and weapons. Bonteboks have a prominent white facial patch and a white rump and belly. They are all white below the knees. The remainder of the body is a rich reddish brown. The horns are curved and deeply ridged or ringed, making these animals prized by trophy hunters.

AFRICAN WILD ASSES have also been the victims of guns. Herdsmen claim they eat more grass than goats do and have tried to exterminate these progenitors of the domestic donkey. But large herds of grazing domestic goats do more damage to the environment than these animals do.

There are two subspecies of African Wild Ass: the Nubian and the Somali. Each has been reduced to a few hundred animals. In some areas the wild asses have inter-bred with domestic donkeys, resulting in a loss of their original purebred identity. It would be a great pity to lose either of these subspecies, for these little animals can thrive in remote areas and are part of the natural balance there.

Arabian Oryx

Bontebok

African
Wild Ass

49

FORESTS

The world's largest forest circles the earth in the Northern Hemisphere in a broad belt commencing just south of the tundra. It consists almost wholly of needle-leaved trees, such as pines, hemlocks, firs, spruces, and other conifers. Along its northernmost fringe, the trees straggle into the tundra, dwarfed and wind-warped in their efforts to grow in the cold land. Everywhere the forest has a sameness of appearance. Where the trees form a dense forest, a thick carpet of needles has built up on the floor over the centuries, and a gray soil has slowly formed.

In Europe this forest, called the *taiga,* occupies a vast lowland created during the Great Ice Age. The glacial ice gouged deeply in many places to form bogs, swamps, ponds, and lakes. In North America the coniferous forest

Coniferous forest with glacial pond.

covers most of Canada, with its tendrils extending into the hardwood deciduous forest region of the central United States and even farther south along mountain ridges.

Winters are long in this region, lasting from six months on its southern fringes to as long as nine months along the tundra. Plants grow and produce their seeds rapidly in the short summers. In this brief period, too, animals must find food that will help them get through the winter months, when food becomes scarce. Some animals migrate from the region in winter; others hibernate. Many insects enter a dormant stage in their life cycle. But some kinds of animals remain active all winter. As in summer, they feed on the seeds in the pinecones, or they eat bark or needles. And every herbivore is a potential meal for some carnivore.

Coniferous northern forests are the world's greatest source of timber. Harvesting of the trees has not always been managed wisely, however. Too often there has been total destruction over a wide area, disrupting or destroying wildlife populations. Even so, these great northern forests are some of the least disturbed of the world's large habitats, especially in North America. Many animals that once ranged widely throughout the north and in the temperate zones remain now only in the "North Woods."

South of these coniferous forests were once extensive woodlands of deciduous trees such as oaks, hickories, maples, poplars, and others that shed their leaves in winter. Huge forests of these trees were once widespread in temperate regions of North America, Europe, and Asia, but long ago they fell to the saw and the ax. With them went many species of wildlife, for this became the most heavily settled region of the world. Here are most of the world's

Farm fields with deciduous forest on right.

great cities and towns, and the open areas between them are either farmed or broken up into smaller living tracts.

Along the equator and immediately to its north and south are the world's evergreen rainforests. There the rainfall is no less than 80 inches annually—and much more in a narrow belt near the equator. One rainforest, for example, regularly gets about 400 inches of rain every year and sometimes more. Throughout most of the tropics and subtropics, the rain comes all in one season. For the remaining months—the dry season—there may be little or no rain. At the edges of the tropics and with the climate controlled largely by the prevailing winds, the jungle grades into deciduous trees or into thorny shrubs. Along the seacoasts are dense mangrove thickets.

The abundance of rain and the year-round warmth—the temperature in a tropical rainforest ranges from a high of about 100° F to a low of about 70° F—result in a great variety of animals and plants. Literally hundreds of species of trees may be found in a small area, while a deciduous forest of the same size in temperate climates, for example, will contain only a dozen or so species. A northern coniferous forest contains only one or two.

When a tropical rainforest is mature, the tall trees form an almost solid canopy 100 feet or more off the ground, blocking out the sunlight. For this reason the floor of a tropical rainforest is usually bare of plants, or nearly so, except at its edges, where the sun can reach the ground. Many woody vines, or lianas, lace their way through the tallest trees, which may also be filled with clumps of plants called epiphytes, which live on the tree branches and have no root connection to the ground below.

Cold-blooded animals tend to reach their largest size in the tropics. Here, for example, are the giants among the snakes, crocodiles, toads, and moths. Most warm-blooded animals, in contrast, are smaller than their nearest relatives that live in temperate-climate regions.

53

The canopy of a South American rainforest, showing epiphytes, lianas, and a Common Brazilian Marmoset.

Food is plentiful, but almost all of the fruits as well as the foliage are high above the forest floor. To get to them, an animal must either fly or climb. Modes of travel in a rainforest include every imaginable variation, from that of slow-creeping sloths (which, while hanging upside down, sluggishly make their way along the underside of branches) to that of the much swifter, more agile gibbons and other primates. Hovering hummingbirds sip nectar from deep-throated flowers while still on the wing, and big-billed toucans and hornbills feed on fruit. Some tree-dwelling frogs glide from tree to tree using parachutelike webs between their toes, and slim snakes slip noiselessly and arrowlike from branch to branch. Many jungle animals are born in the trees and never descend to the ground at all.

Though teeming with life, tropical rainforests are also extremely fragile. Their most abundant resources are the

rain and the warm sunshine. In an undisturbed forest either canopied high above the ground or covered with dense vegetation lower down—the fall of the rain is broken, and the sunlight is filtered before reaching the earth. But where jungles have been cleared for farming or for harvesting timber, this process is interrupted. Disturbed, too, is the thick litter containing important kinds of fungi that hasten the decomposing and recycling of nutrients. The soil itself is poor, for about 80 percent of the nutrients in the jungle are either in the growing plants or in the forest litter.

Jungles are usually cleared for farming by the primitive technique of cutting and burning all the vegetation. This is fast, but it also destroys the reservoirs of nutrients. Crops usually grow well for only one or two seasons; the pioneer farmers then have to move on to new land. There they repeat their slash-and-burn devastation again, leaving

55

behind a greatly depleted soil—one that is less rich than that of many desert lands. When attempts are made to prolong the use of the land, such as by adding chemical fertilizers, the heavy rains leach the nutrients from the soil before the crop plants can derive any benefit. A forest will eventually grow again, but many centuries must pass before a multistoried jungle reappears.

Although the tropics are rich with a tremendous variety of life, the number of individuals in a species is generally less here than in other regions. If hunters and collectors concentrate their efforts on a particular species, such as an especially colorful parrot that has become popular as a pet or a cat that provides a much-sought-after pelt, a whole population of a species can disappear in a very short time. The human populations in the rainforests may not be sensitive to worldwide environmental problems. They need food— often desperately. If a parrot brings them money that will put food on the table or provide for other basic needs, there is no question about it: the parrot is destined for a cage.

A large portion of South America lies in the tropics, which consist mostly of the great basin of the Amazon River—an area almost as large as the United States. Based on the volume of water it carries, the Amazon is the largest river in the world, flowing eastward for 4,000 miles from its Pacific headwaters in the Peruvian Andes. The delta of the Amazon is 200 miles wide, a huge depository for silt from the river's 500 or so tributaries. Although one of the least developed wilderness areas in the world, the Amazon tropics are also in great danger. Thousands of acres are being destroyed every hour of every day.

Africa's tropical forests are much smaller in total area than South America's, but the problems in Africa are also great because of the long-range impact of people in the region. The forested areas of Africa are confined almost wholly to the tropical west coast.

The destruction of the world's tropical rainforests continues unabated, in spite of large-scale efforts to halt it.

Asia's tropics include the most heavily populated areas of the world, yet there are still dense and uninhabited jungles in the lowlands of India, Burma, Cambodia, and South Vietnam. In these areas, people and wildlife are in constant conflict, and the wildlife is usually the loser. Starving people are understandably rarely sympathetic to the plight of wild animals, and so those concerned with the saving of wildlife must first attend to the welfare of humans.

CAROLINA PARAKEETS were once abundant in the woodlands of the southern United States. They were killed for sport and also because they made pests of themselves by eating the seeds of fruits and other crops. The last of these parakeets are believed to have died in the Florida Everglades in the 1920s. A caged bird died in 1918 in the Cincinnati Zoo, where it had lived alongside the last of the Passenger Pigeons. But unlike the Passenger Pigeon, the handsome Carolina Parakeet, with its metallic green body, yellow neck, and orange to crimson crown, got almost no attention. Have we really lost the little bird? A small flock was reported seen in South Carolina in the 1930s.

Carolina Parakeet

HEATH HENS were relatives of prairie chickens but lived in the woodlands and scrub oak plains. Heath Hens were once so common in North America that they almost became a staple of the colonists' diet. Dogs and cats ate many of these ground-nesting birds, too.

Heath Hen

Eventually it became clear that the Heath Hen population was dwindling. Laws passed to protect the birds were not enforced. By the early 1900s the survivors, a hundred or so, were all confined to a preserve on Martha's Vineyard, off Cape Cod in Massachusetts. The flock grew to several thousand. A series of natural disasters then occurred— first a devastating fire, followed soon after by an uncommonly cold winter. The hapless flock was once again reduced to about a hundred birds, which were easily captured by predators in the fire-cleared land. Disease followed, and in 1932 the last of the Heath Hens died.

Ivory-billed
Woodpecker

Red-cockaded
Woodpecker

IVORY-BILLED WOODPECKERS of the deciduous forest regions in the southeastern United States and Cuba were black and white with a bright red crest on their head. They were the largest (more than 1½ feet long) and most striking species of North American woodpecker. Only the very similar Pileated Woodpecker approached them in size.

Unfortunately, the bird's diet was highly specialized. It fed mainly on the grubs (larvae) of wood-boring beetles living in dead oak, ash, pine, and cypress trees. As forests were leveled, there were fewer dead trees, which are produced only by mature forests.

The Ivory-billed Woodpecker was never abundant, but it might have been spared extinction by providing it with suitable sanctuaries. A retreat of precisely this sort was established for them in a northern Florida forest, one of several such places where sightings of the birds had been made in recent years. But it is now widely believed that the bird's plight was recognized too late and that it has disappeared.

The Imperial Woodpecker, which once lived in the oak and pine forests on mountain slopes in Mexico, was a similar-looking but slightly larger close relative of the Ivory-billed Woodpecker. That species is now either extinct or nearly so.

The Red-cockaded Woodpecker, which inhabits forests of Longleaf Pines in the southeastern United States, is now endangered. Nearly all of the remaining birds are found only in national forests, where there are large stands of mature trees.

59

Passenger Pigeon

PASSENGER PIGEONS once existed in North America in vast numbers. The females laid only one egg a year, but until people invaded their world, this was enough to sustain the birds and build huge flocks, some of which are said to have contained as many as 50 million birds. In flight they darkened the skies—literally blotting out the sun—as they passed overhead. Nothing but birds could be seen from horizon to horizon.

Wherever these gigantic flocks nested or stopped to roost in the evening, they broke the branches from the trees, and their droppings whitened the ground below them like fresh snow. One nesting colony was estimated to have been 50 miles wide and about 250 miles long.

In earlier days, of course, no one gave any thought to the need to protect the Passenger Pigeon. People felt they were eliminating what they considered to be a pest while at the same time obtaining food for their tables. An ambitious hunter could kill as many as 10,000 birds in one day, and there were many hunters. Millions of Passenger Pigeons were slaughtered for sale in markets. They were hauled to New York and other big cities by the hundreds of tons. Hogs were also fattened on their carcasses.

The massacre went on year after year until at last the massive flocks were reduced to scattered groups. Even in the late 1800s, however, proposed legislation to protect the Passenger Pigeon was not passed because lawmakers believed that the birds were still too abundant and too prolific to be in any real danger of extermination.

Perhaps even more damaging to the Passenger Pigeon was the destruction of its woodland habitat. These birds were highly adapted to living in deciduous forests, where they nested and also got most of their food. By the 1890s the Passenger Pigeon had become so scarce that it was no longer profitable to hunt the birds commercially. In addition, the remaining birds simply could not produce enough offspring to replace themselves. A few birds were seen—and promptly shot—in the early 1900s, and then they were gone.

The very last Passenger Pigeon on earth, a female named Martha, was kept in a cage in the Cincinnati Zoo, where she had hatched from an egg some thirty years earlier. She died there in 1914, never having flown with a flock of her own kind. She was the last survivor of what once might have been the world's most abundant bird.

Bald Eagle

BALD EAGLES once flew over most of North America. Today their remnant populations are concentrated mostly in southern Alaska. Primarily fish eaters, Bald Eagles live mainly along seacoasts or around large lakes. Powerful birds with keen eyesight, they swoop down from the sky to snatch prey in their sharp, hooked talons. They may also pilfer fish caught by other birds.

For a number of years the Bald Eagle was declining at such an alarming rate that its total demise seemed inevitable. Pesticides—most specifically DDT—were to blame. The Bald Eagles picked up small doses of the poison from virtually every fish they ate. These small amounts accumulated in their body and caused the females to lay weak-shelled eggs that broke before hatching. Much of the large bird's original habitat was destroyed, too, and many birds were killed either to obtain their feathers for use as ornaments or to eliminate the birds as potential threats to livestock. With DDT banned since 1972 and also with greater protection, Bald Eagle populations are slowly building in wilderness areas that can support them.

Spotted Owl

SPOTTED OWLS have never been abundant, but no other owl has stirred up more controversy. Standing less than 2 feet tall and weighing only about 2 pounds, this fluffy little bird became listed as an endangered species in 1989. Its last strongholds are the old-growth forests of the Pacific Northwest, and its endangered status at least temporarily assures the holdup of timber cutting on millions of acres of land owned by the U.S. Forest Service. Environmentalists say this is the only way to spare the species from extinction. Many members of the timber industry disagree.

TINAMOUS are small, grouselike birds that inhabit the forests and grasslands of Central and South America. Some of the 40 or so species have been heavily hunted, but loss of habitat is the greatest threat. Two forest dwellers—Peru's Black-headed Tinamou and Venezuela's Barred Tinamou—are among the world's rarest and least known birds.

RED-BILLED CURASSOWS are among some 40 species of forest-dwelling pheasantlike birds of the American tropics. The Red-billed Curassow is found in Brazil and is listed as endangered. Another species—the Chachalaca—ranges into the state of Texas. Curassows are becoming extremely rare throughout their range, due both to hunting and to the destruction of their habitat.

Red-billed Curassow

Variegated
Tinamou

PARROTS AND PARAKEETS range in size from no more than 4 inches to 3½ feet tall. Native to tropical and subtropical regions around the world, they have been greatly reduced in number in fairly recent years as a result of habitat loss and the demand for them as pets. Few parrots or parakeets have ever been abundant except locally, and so the population of a particular species can be reduced quickly to a critical low. As an example, only a single Spix's Macaw has been seen in the wild in Brazil in recent years, but there are about 27 in captivity. These handsome birds sell for as much as $60,000 each.

One of the rarest and most unusual of the parrots is the nearly flightless and nocturnal Kakapo, or Owl Parrot. It lives in New Zealand in a small forested and hilly area where it nests in burrows or holes among tree roots. Although it apparently once inhabited nearly all of New Zealand, it was becoming rare even before the arrival of the Europeans and has continued to decrease drastically in number. Introduced predators, such as rats, cats, dogs, and pigs, as well as destruction of its natural habitat, are the main causes.

Kakapo, or Owl Parrot

Kirtland's
Warbler

KIRTLAND'S WARBLER is one of the rarest birds in North America. This yellow-breasted, gray-backed little warbler spends its summers in the pine forests of Michigan and winters in the Bahamas. As the forests where the warbler nested were cleared, the Brown-headed Cowbird became more abundant.

Female cowbirds often lay their eggs in the warblers' nests, then leave the chore of incubating the eggs and rearing the young up to the warblers. The warblers' young, if any do hatch, are either crowded out of the nest or are starved to death because the young cowbird is larger and more demanding. The result is healthy, well-fed cowbirds— and no warblers.

In the dense forests that Kirtland's Warbler once enjoyed, the Brown-headed Cowbird did not exist. Recognizing this, the U.S. Forest Service set aside 4,000 acres of forestland in Michigan as a place for the warblers to nest, but help may have come too late. Some experts say the little warbler is doomed to become extinct within a few years.

THREE-TOED SLOTHS have a well-deserved reputation for slowness. A Three-toed Sloth travels only about 12 feet per minute—when in a hurry. On the ground, dragging itself along clumsily, it can manage only 6 feet or so per minute. Although it is a surprisingly good swimmer, most of its life is spent hanging from branches, and its brownish fur becomes green with growths of algae. Underneath these coarse hairs is a short, soft undercoat. When a sloth dies, it may continue to hang from a branch, hooked in place with its long, curved claws.

The Three-toed Sloth has a special fondness for the fruit and leaves of Cecropia trees, and it may spend its entire life in one tree. The cutting down of the tropical forests has seriously endangered these slowest of all mammals. They have no place else to go, and at the rate they travel they would never get there anyhow.

KOALAS feed only on leaves of eucalyptus, or gum, trees. The Koala does not drink water, and in the language of the aborigines, its name means "no drink." These tree-dwelling marsupials are among the most famous of all Australian animals and have been pursued for their pelts for years. At one time millions of skins were sold every year. A few Koalas are kept in zoos that are able to provide eucalyptus leaves in quantity. Fortunately, Koalas do breed in captivity, and so the species may survive. The Australian government has also established preserves where Koalas are slowly increasing in numbers.

NUMBATS, which are also known as Banded Anteaters, are squirrel-sized marsupials native to Australia. Their reddish back contains half a dozen or so white or off-white bars, and their muzzle ends in a small mouth from which a long, slender tongue is flicked out to pick up crawling termites, their principal food. Numbats live in hollow logs, often ones that have been channeled out initially by termites. They sleep during the night and are active during the day. The cutting down of the forests and frequent attacks by dogs, cats, and foxes have put them on the endangered list. There are two subspecies—the Numbat and the even less abundant Rusty Numbat.

Three-toed Sloth

Koala

Numbat

BATS are the only mammals with wings and thus the capability of true flight. About one in four mammal species in the world is a bat, ranking bats next to rodents in abundance. They can be found everywhere in the world except in the polar regions, on remote oceanic islands, and on ice-capped mountains, but they are most numerous in warm climates.

Some kinds of bats are strictly fruit and nectar eaters. These bats, which have large eyes and good vision, are also the largest, some with wingspans of 5 feet. Two kinds of bats eat fish exclusively. They make their catches by swooping down from above and snatching the fish out of the water. The greatest number of bats, however, are insect eaters. These are the mouse-sized bats commonly seen on their feeding flights on warm evenings in temperate climates. Typically they roost in hollow trees, under rock ledges, in the attics of buildings, or in similarly protected and out-of-the-way places during the day. Some of them migrate to warmer climates in winter while others hibernate, often congregating in uncountable thousands in caves.

Bats are generally not popular with people. Most have small eyes and wrinkled pug faces. The wrinkles serve as sound traps, for bats navigate and also search for food by echolocation. This consists of emitting high-pitched sounds beyond the range of human hearing. These sound pulses bounce off anything in their path and are picked up as echoes by the bats' sensitive ears.

A number of species of bats are currently endangered, due primarily to destruction of their habitat. In the central United States, as an example, the woodland-loving Gray Bat inhabiting the middle of the continent is now listed as an endangered species. Once it was one of the most abundant mammals in its range, but its population has been reduced to an estimated million. The bats are no longer safe even in caves. Human visitors cause the females to drop their young

Gray Bat

to the cave floor, where they are attacked and eaten by mice or are drowned in pools of water. There is a critical low from which a population of animals is no longer capable of recovering, and scientists are concerned that this point may soon be reached by many beleaguered bat species. Areas of cut-over forests are being restored to help the bats make a comeback, and roost areas are being marked as "off limits" for visitors.

Aside from a simple desire not to harm any living creature that does not do us any harm, why should we preserve these unusual little animals? For one thing, because many species are insect eaters. A single Gray Bat, for example, will eat as many as a thousand insects every night. A colony of these bats will consume as many as a million insects in one night. In addition, many bat species are important pollinators and seed dispersers for commercially important crops in tropical forest and savanna habitats. Thus, they are indeed a significant part of nature's natural balance.

69

Red Wolf

RED WOLVES were, until very recently, believed doomed. Once they roamed over most of the central and southern United States, but they were forced to retreat as the land was settled. The Timber, or Gray, Wolf, which once ranged widely over temperate regions of the Northern Hemisphere, moved northward, where the remaining animals survive principally in the "North Woods." The smaller Red Wolf moved southward, nearer to civilization. Those that escaped guns and poisoned baits live in the shrunken wilderness areas of Louisiana, Arkansas, Texas, and Mexico. The actual number of survivors is not known. Those few kept in captivity have been bred, however, and their offspring are being returned to those wilderness areas that can support them.

70

The Red Wolf may not actually be a true species. Some geneticists say it may instead be a natural hybrid of the Timber Wolf and the Coyote. If this is eventually proved correct, the hybrid Red Wolf may not be protected under the Endangered Species Act, since only purebreds—true species—supposedly qualify for these funds.

JAGUARS are the largest cats native to the American tropics. Like leopards, they are spotted, but their spots consist of a black spot surrounded by a yellowish or lighter circle and then an outer circle of black, forming a rosette. Jaguars range in color from yellowish to almost wholly black. They hunt at night and rest in secluded spots during the day, mostly staying in lowland areas near streams and lakes. The cutting down of forests has forced them to retreat to ever-smaller tracts, and they have been hunted both for their pelts and to eliminate them in areas where people fear their presence or their attacks on livestock. They are now one of the world's most endangered animals.

Jaguar

71

TIGERS at one time ranged widely across Asia, and like other big cats, they have long been in conflict with humans, whom they do sometimes attack. But with guns, people have had the longest and most lethal reach. Poaching to obtain tiger bones for use in primitive medicines has added to the problem. In the last few decades, the total number of tigers has been reduced from some 100,000 to about 8,000. Those few remaining animals must be given protection to prevent extermination of the species.

Some tigers do kill cattle and have also taken a toll of people—perhaps several hundred per year in the recent past, up to a thousand per year before that. People have retaliated. However, hunts are sometimes organized as much for sport as to get rid of a particular miscreant. And not all tigers are man eaters. Often it is an older tiger that can no longer capture wild prey that goes after people.

Tigers are the largest of the living cats, with big males commonly weighing more than 500 pounds. The Siberian Tiger, which lives in the north, has a longer and paler coat than does the Bengal Tiger of the tropics.

Bengal Tiger

Puma

PUMAS, also known as Cougars, Mountain Lions, Panthers, and at least a dozen other names, were once the most widely distributed large mammals in North America. They ranged from southern Canada to the southern tip of South America and were equally at home in the tropics, deserts, and mountains, with a preference for forested areas.

A Puma may measure nearly 9 feet from the tip of its nose to the tip of its tail and weigh well over 200 pounds. Females are about a third smaller than males. Pumas usually prey on deer or other large animals, but a hungry animal will not turn down smaller prey, even a mouse. As the land became settled, some cats attacked livestock, and soon the full wrath of humans was turned against the cats. Bounties were offered, and some men became hired killers of these handsome animals. Thousands of Pumas were exterminated, and it is remarkable that any still exist today.

The few thousand remaining creatures are confined largely to wilderness areas in Florida and the mountains in the West. They avoid human beings whenever possible but can be tamed and will breed in captivity.

Leopard
with prey

LEOPARDS are big cats that live in the jungles of Africa and Asia. They are also found in grasslands, brush country, deserts, arid savannas, and even near urban areas. Some range into the high mountains. Those living in the lowlands typically have dark yellow coats marked with black rosette-shaped spots. Wholly black forms, more common in dense, moist forests, are sometimes called panthers.

Considering the popularity of their pelts for coats and other apparel, leopards have fared surprisingly well. However, they are still shot at for attacking livestock, which they sometimes do when their natural prey is scarce.

Snow Leopards, which are a separate species from Leopards, number only about 500 in the wild. They live at the edge of the snow line in the mountains of central Asia. At these high elevations—from 5,000 to 15,000 feet—they manage to avoid people.

The wary Snow Leopard is prized for its soft gray pelt spotted with black. Like Leopards, it can make spectacular leaps—to as much as 30 feet horizontally and 12 feet vertically. Snow Leopards do breed readily in captivity. But they are very sensitive to heat, and special accommodations must be made for keeping them.

The Clouded Leopard, which is also not a true Leopard, lives at lower elevations and is more abundant. But it is still endangered, due to habitat loss and hunting for its pelt. Clouded Leopards are about 6 feet long, including their long tail. Like Snow Leopards, Clouded Leopards do well in captivity. Their status in the wild, however, is uncertain.

MARGAYS AND OCELOTS are small, handsome cats of the American tropics that have been hunted for their pelts and meat. Also, much of their forest habitat has disappeared as a result of encroaching civilization. Although their populations are not easily determined with accuracy, these cats are known to be endangered.

Ocelot

Margay

TAPIRS are shy and retiring creatures that look like a type of pig because of their long snout but are really more closely related to rhinoceroses and horses. Tapirs live mainly along waterways. Three species are found in Central and South America and one in Malaysia. Both the Mountain Tapir and Baird's Tapir live in South America's mountain forests up to elevations of more than 12,000 feet. The Brazilian Tapir and the Malayan Tapir inhabit tropical lowlands. A mature Brazilian Tapir may weigh as much as 800 pounds; other species weigh less.

Tapirs have never been abundant and are now endangered. They have long been a favorite food of most large predators and have also been hunted heavily by humans. Most damaging, however, has been the destruction of their habitat. Long ago their range included North America, but now they are found only in the tropics. However, that world is fast disappearing, too. Tapirs may be spared by the establishment of parks and reservations and by the fact that they do reasonably well in captivity.

DUIKERS are short-legged forest-dwelling antelopes of central and southern Africa. All of the roughly dozen species are rather small, some only about 2 feet long. Usually they travel alone or in pairs. Most are secretive and also rare, due partly to the destruction of the forests and savannas where they live; some, however, exist in large numbers even in settled areas. Their name is Dutch for "diver" and refers to the speedy way these shy little antelopes can literally dive out of sight into the underbrush.

OKAPIS, which live in the jungles of Zaire, are close relatives of giraffes but have short necks and stand only about 5 feet tall at the shoulder. Like giraffes, they have skin-covered knoblike horns, and they use their tongues to pluck leaves from trees. Their legs have white stripes, like a zebra's, but

Malayan Tapir

Okapi

Striped-backed Duiker

their bodies are velvety dark chestnut to almost purplish black. Most surprising, these rather large animals were not discovered until 1901. Early attempts to capture them failed, but in 1918 the first ones were trapped, and in the 1930s several were reared in captivity. These animals have given birth to young, but the Okapi is still considered rare and has been protected in Zaire since 1933.

PÈRE DAVID'S DEER is named for the French missionary who discovered the deer in about 1860 on a royal game preserve near Beijing (Peking). When he was refused official entry to the preserve, he bribed guards to allow him to climb over the high stone wall surrounding it. Inside he saw more than a hundred strange deer that he was told no longer existed in the wild. Determined to get specimens for scientists in Europe, he once again bribed guards and soon had two skins to send to Europe. The Chinese government then relented and sent three live animals, which unfortunately died during their journey. But the skins and the specimens were enough to establish the deer as a new species.

Zoos in Europe soon clamored for Père David's Deer to exhibit, and the Chinese government responded to this by sending them more than a dozen. The deer bred well in captivity, and their offspring were sent to other zoos. Meanwhile disaster struck the herd in China. A flood swept away the wall around the preserve. Only a few dozen deer could be rounded up after the flood waters subsided, and these were killed and eaten by soldiers during a rebellion. Many of those not kept in pairs died in European zoos.

A wealthy sportsman had been purchasing "extra" animals from the zoos over the years to keep on his estate, and he began returning animals to the zoos. There are now hundreds of Père David's Deer in zoos and on preserves. Thus, these strange deer with their long, shaggy tail, goat-like hoofs, and large reindeer-like antlers would not be alive today if the missionary had not been persistent. No one knows how many of these deer lived in the wild originally, but it was undoubtedly encroachment of civilization that eliminated them from their natural habitat.

PYGMY HIPPOPOTAMUSES live in the African jungles, and they have never been abundant. They stand about 2½ feet

78

Père David's Deer

Pygmy Hippopotamus

tall at the shoulders (roughly the size of a domestic pig) and weigh only about 500 pounds. In contrast, the Common Hippopotamus may weigh more than 4 tons! The Pygmy Hippopotamus, which has a narrower snout than its much larger cousin, feeds on vegetation in swamps and on the forest floor. Active only at night, the shy Pygmy Hippo is rarely seen, but hunting and destruction of habitat due to logging may have caused it to become scarce. There are some Pygmy Hippopotamuses in zoos, however, where they readily mate and produce young.

LANGURS (not illustrated) are slender, leaf-eating Asiatic monkeys. Ten years ago, these animals did not do well in captivity, but better knowledge of their nutritional needs has changed that situation. Langurs rarely come to the ground, and they are totally dependent on trees and their leaves for food. It is the cutting of forests that has imperiled them. Among the endangered are the Douc Langur, Pagi Langur, and three species of snub-nosed langurs.

TAMARINS are handsome monkeys that live mainly in the rainforests of Brazil. All are squirrel-sized, and in most species the tail is a third longer than the body. Tamarins communicate with shrill calls, twitters, and squeaks. Most species are identified by their distinctive coloration, combined with manes, ruffs, tufts, beards, and other hair adornments. Unfortunately, their natural forest habitats are being destroyed.

Emperor
Tamarin

Black and White
Colobus Monkey

COLOBUS MONKEYS, or guerezas, are leaf eaters that live in Africa. Colobus comes from the Greek word *kolobos*, which means "mutilated," and it refers to the monkeys' small but nonfunctional thumb. All four species are hunted for their handsome, thick, and silky pelts and for food. They are also threatened by the destruction of the forests in which they live. Those with black-and-white pelts have been hunted most intensively.

81

GORILLAS, the largest and most powerful of the primates, are rapidly becoming scarce. Only a few hundred Mountain Gorillas still survive in tropical Africa. Other subspecies are more numerous but still endangered. Their disappearance is due mostly to hunting and destruction of their habitat.

Gorillas are truly giants. Males may stand about 6 feet tall, weigh up to 400 pounds, and have an arm spread of about 8 feet. Females are about half this size. Gorillas have a huge head and prominent ridges over their eyes. Their body is covered with a dense coat of black hair, but their upper chest, hands, face, and feet are bare.

Gorillas usually walk on all fours, with their fists clenched and their knuckles touching the ground. They are skilled climbers but forage mostly on the ground. Gorillas live in troops of about a dozen animals, led by a dominating older, graying male called a silverback. Females and young sleep in low tree branches. Since gorillas are strictly vegetarian, their raids on crops often bring them into conflict with humans. Their main hope for survival lies in parks and reservations set aside for them as habitats.

Woolly Spider Monkey

SPIDER MONKEYS and the Red-backed Squirrel Monkey, both found in Central American tropical rainforests, plus the Woolly Spider Monkey of southeastern Brazil, are also on the brink of extinction. Mostly, they have been victims of habitat destruction. The natives also hunt them for food.

Red
Uakari

Gorilla

UAKARIS are the only short-tailed monkeys living in the Americas. They are found in the tropics, primarily in tree-tops alongside rivers or lakes, and rarely come to the ground. Both of the two existing species have no hair at all on their face or the top of their head. The face of one species is bright red. The face of the other is black. Coat colors range from white to reddish brown with black to brown and black. Both species are endangered. Uakaris eat mostly fruits but probably also eat leaves, insects, and other small animals. Rather quiet monkeys, they are most active during the day and can move fast on all fours.

83

RHESUS MONKEYS have the misfortune of being suscep-
tible to many diseases that also plague humans, and so they
have been used extensively in medical research. They also
do well and breed in captivity. Several species associate
closely with humans. Rhesus monkeys have been known to
live in urban areas in India. In their natural habitat, they are
now rare.

Rhesus monkeys are members of the macaque family, a
widely distributed group of Asiatic monkeys. In troops made
up of a few dozen to as many as several hundred individuals, they sleep in trees at night but frequently come down to
the forest floor to forage for food or travel to a new territory.
A number of macaques in addition to the rhesus have been
studied intensively and used in research. Capturing them for
this purpose has contributed greatly to their population
decline, as has the destruction of their natural habitat.

Rhesus Monkeys

STREAMS, LAKES, AND WETLANDS

Of all the water on earth, only about 2 percent is fresh, and more than half of this is permanently locked in snow or ice in the polar regions or on high mountains. Less than 1 percent is found in streams, lakes, and wetlands. Yet these waterways are very significant environments for life.

Compared to the oceans, fresh water is much less uniform in its physical and chemical characteristics. Great differences in oxygen content, amount of food, light, temperature, and other factors occur not only from one body of water to another but also in the same body of water at different times of the day and from season to season. Some streams flow swiftly; others are sluggish. Some lakes are deep and cold; others are warm and shallow. As a result of these variations, the kinds of living things inhabiting fresh waters are extremely varied.

Since the beginning, people have favored living along or near streams and lakes, which have provided them with food and water, served as transportation routes, and—of increasing importance in recent years—offered places for recreation. Almost all of the food and nutrient cycles of fresh waters are linked to the land, and so whatever is done to the land affects the life in these waters.

Abuses of the land are quickly made evident by streams, lakes, and wetlands. Streams become open sewers; lakes become cesspools or catch basins. In the United States many major river systems are now polluted—so much so that a few can no longer support almost any sort of life. Cities and industries are not the only polluters. Some of the most damaging pollution comes from agriculture. Fertilizers and insecticides, applied to crops and also to forest areas, eventually find their way into streams, lakes, and wetlands. Directly or indirectly, they kill fish and their prey and also birds and other predators that feed on fish.

The spraying of pesticides has seriously threatened the ecology of the wetlands.

Silt, consisting mostly of valuable topsoil eroded from the land, washes into streams and lakes or is carried to the open sea. Many thousands of acres of irreplaceable topsoil in the United States alone are lost every day, with the land becoming increasingly nutrient-poor. The silt also robs the water of oxygen, creating unfavorable conditions for many plants and other forms of marine life and settling over the bottom in a thick, choking ooze.

Wetlands soak up water like sponges, releasing it very slowly into the surrounding land. Frogs, toads, turtles, and snakes, as well as fish and other aquatic animals, live in wetlands. Muskrats, mink, and other small mammals inhabit wetlands, too, as do many kinds of birds. Ducks and geese use wetlands as nesting sites.

Fish are not included in this book, but like frogs and other amphibians, they are highly vulnerable to changes in their world of water. More than a third of the world's endangered animals are fish. Obviously, the aquatic world is rapidly becoming a perilous place—faster, in fact, than any other major habitat.

A Green Heron stands watch over this healthy wetlands ecosystem.

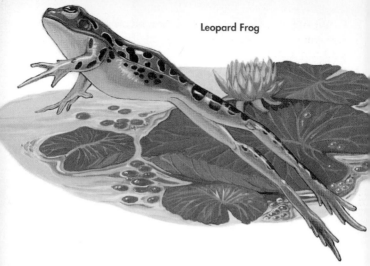

Leopard Frog

LEOPARD FROGS were once abundant along streams, lakes, and ponds throughout most of North America. Now they are rare. Countless thousands were used every year for dissection to study anatomy in biology classes. Others were hunted for food, their legs considered a delicacy. Contributing most to their demise has been the destruction of their habitat, however. Many of the waters along which they lived and in which their young developed have been drained and no longer exist, and others are now dangerously polluted.

The watery world of all amphibians (frogs, toads, salamanders, and newts) is fragile. A census of these animals is difficult because of their small size and their secretive habits. It is known, however, that the populations of nearly all amphibians are diminishing at an alarming rate and that many are doomed to extinction. This is indeed a bad omen, for amphibians are key indicators of what is happening to the total environment.

GHARIALS, often called *Gavials* due to an old clerical error, are slim-snouted crocodilian reptiles that inhabit the rivers and brackish waters of India. The males use a knobby protuberance on top of their snout to amplify their snorting bellows. Evidence indicates that Gharials may once have reached a length of 30 feet, but about 20 feet is maximum today. So many were killed by hunters that a few years ago the Gharial population was believed to be under a hundred. Given protection in special sanctuaries, and also with eggs hatched and young reared in captivity, the population of Gharials has grown to several thousand.

Gharial

ALLIGATORS are among the earth's most feared creatures. There are only two living species of this reptile. The Chinese Alligator, which lives in the Yangtze River, apparently inspired the widely used dragon motif in China. In the early 1900s this alligator was thought to be extinct. Then in the 1930s a few were discovered living in a remote area, and while its situation in the wild is again unknown, the Chinese Alligator has thrived and bred successfully in captivity.

American Alligators are much larger, known to reach a length of 20 feet in the past though rarely exceeding 15 feet today. They were so abundant in Florida in the early days that explorers said they could walk across rivers on the backs of the big beasts. Millions of alligators were killed throughout the lower southeastern United States, some

American Alligator

simply because people did not want to share living space with them. Others were used as food, with their thick tail cut up into steaks. Countless baby alligators were captured and sold as pets.

However, most American Alligators were slaughtered for the smooth but tough skin on their bellies, which was turned into wallets, belts, shoes, purses, luggage, and other durable leather items. The skin on the alligator's back, covered with thick horny plates, was considered worthless.

The American Alligator was annihilated in many areas, and for a time its survival was in doubt. Then protective laws were passed and strictly enforced, resulting in the American Alligator making a dramatic comeback. Controlled hunting is now used to keep its population in check.

EGRETS had the misfortune of sporting handsome plumes that became fashionable to use on hats and other garments. In the United States both the Snowy Egret and the Common Egret were hunted to near extinction. Hundreds of thousands of the big birds were slaughtered. The killing of a National Audubon Society warden by a plume hunter focused attention on the birds' plight, and laws were soon passed to ban the commercial use of the plumes. With the market eliminated, hunters lost interest. Now both birds are becoming abundant again and serve as encouraging examples of recovery when threats are eliminated.

SNAIL KITES originally ranged over all of Florida and may still be found southward through Cuba and Mexico into northern South America. Today, however, the Snail Kite is everywhere either extremely rare or endangered, a victim of humans having destroyed its specialized food source.

The Snail Kite eats mainly the plump apple snail, using its slim, sickle-shaped bill to extract the morsels from the shell. In Florida, as wetlands have been drained, most of the snails have disappeared or been forced into drainage canals or ditches, where they have become infested with flukes. When a Snail Kite eats an infested snail, it also becomes infested with flukes; this can kill the bird.

In the United States the Snail Kite appears to be doomed, even though attempts have been made to provide it with suitable sanctuaries. The chances of its surviving in Central and South America are somewhat better, at least for the time being; but there, too, it will probably disappear as additional wetlands are drained. To prosper, both the bird and its snail food need large tracts of marshy land. The decision must be made whether the land is needed more for people or for this highly specialized bird. Of course, this same land is also of great importance to the survival of many other kinds of wildlife.

Snowy Egret

Common Egret

Snail Kites

93

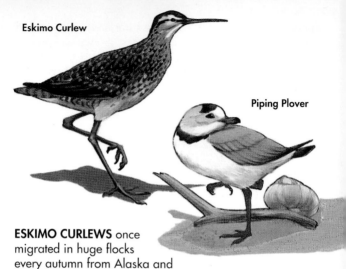

Eskimo Curlew

Piping Plover

ESKIMO CURLEWS once migrated in huge flocks every autumn from Alaska and Canada to South America, then returned in the spring. Their round trip covered some 8,000 miles—and all along the way they encountered hunters. By 1900 the great flocks were gone. In fact, the bird was thought to be extinct until a few were seen again recently. It is possible that the Eskimo Curlew is making a comeback, particularly now that it is protected by law in the United States and Canada.

PIPING PLOVERS were never abundant, but they were seen with regularity along the beaches of the eastern United States. Those who know them appreciate their melodious calls. Now the Piping Plover is rare. It is estimated that fewer than 5,000 exist today. Their demise is due to the destruction of their nesting sites along beaches where people have built houses and other structures. Also contributing are the hordes of beachgoers who disrupt the birds' critical nesting and rearing period in the summer. Many eggs and hatchlings are trampled by people or run over by vehicles roving the beach. Some sections of beach are now being fenced and even patrolled to give the birds the privacy and protection they will need for survival. These efforts seem to be resulting in a slow increase in the Piping Plover's population.

BACHMAN'S WARBLERS are very rare North American songbirds. Some experts think they were already headed toward extinction when they were first discovered in South Carolina by naturalist John Bachman in 1833. Their choice of habitat is moist woodlands. The few remaining birds are making a last stand in swampy areas along rivers.

CAPE SABLE SPARROWS are found in extreme southeastern Florida, where only a few hundred are believed to still exist. Most of their habitat was destroyed by real estate developments. Hurricanes have also taken a toll. The Dusky Seaside Sparrow, which once lived in the coastal marshes of central Florida, suffered similarly from its habitat being destroyed by drainage, filling, and development of the land. Sadly, it became extinct in the late 1980s.

Bachman's Warbler

Cape Sable Sparrow

PLATYPUSES are egg-laying mammals (monotremes) that live in lakes and streams in Australia. This unusual species is not now in any real danger. However, because it is so highly specialized, even minor changes in its habitat can put it at risk. Care must be taken if this species is to survive.

The Platypus digs out an underwater burrow that is partly on land. During the day it rests in the above-water section of the burrow. In the early morning and evening, it comes out to feed on crayfish and other small aquatic animals on the stream bottom.

The female lays one or two eggs inside the burrow, in a nest she builds. She sits on this nest for about two weeks. The newly hatched young lap up a milky secretion that flows into pockets on the mother's underside. Unusually, the mother does not have nippled mammary glands.

Until recently the web-footed Platypus was hunted and trapped for its short, dense fur. When it was seen that this unique animal was becoming extremely rare, the government passed laws prohibiting its capture—even for zoo exhibition. With the protection it now has, the Platypus is making a slow but steady comeback.

Platypus

Giant Otter

GIANT OTTERS, which inhabit the rivers of northern South America, may measure more than 6 feet long, their flat and almost beaverlike tail accounting for about a third of this length. A Giant Otter is chocolate brown on the back, lighter on the belly, and streaked with light and dark hairs on the throat and chest. Its head is flat and its neck thick, sometimes broader than the head in older animals. Both front and hind feet are webbed. Underwater, the Giant Otter uses its tail and hind legs to propel itself. Often it floats on its back, like the Sea Otter.

Hunters have cut so deeply into the Giant Otter's population that it is now an endangered species. The trade in otter pelts has been banned, but unfortunately, illegal hunting continues.

OCEANS

The earth is bathed in a solution of salt water that covers about 90 percent of the Southern Hemisphere and 60 percent of the Northern Hemisphere. Hidden beneath the surface are deep canyons, high mountains, broad plains, and powerful currents—all in a scale that makes any comparable features on land seem diminutive. Mount Everest, the highest mountain on earth, towers to 29,141 feet above sea level, but if it were dropped into the Mariannas Trench, the deepest rift in the sea, its top would still be 1½ miles below the surface.

Despite their immensity, the seas offer remarkably uniform conditions for life. The salt content is the same over great expanses, and the temperature typically changes slowly in any given region, differing little from day to day and season to season. Such uniform conditions do not usually result in a great variety of life forms, but individuals of an existing species often occur in prodigious numbers.

Yet this vast ocean world—so much larger than all of the land environments combined—is being despoiled. True, the seas are safe from the plow and the ax, but humans are killing the seas with poisons.

At the base of the food chain in the oceans are plankton, extremely tiny plants and animals that are so abundant in the great "pastures" of open water that they give the sea its characteristic color. As the minuscule one-celled plants manufacture food, they also release oxygen into the atmosphere—one fourth to one third of all free oxygen in the air.

Countless kinds of fish and other creatures feed only on plankton. The Blue Whale, the largest of all sea animals—in fact, the largest animal on earth—is a plankton eater, as are the Whale Shark and several other giants of the open sea. The great schools of herring on which entire nations depend are also based on plankton. Many plankton feeders, in turn,

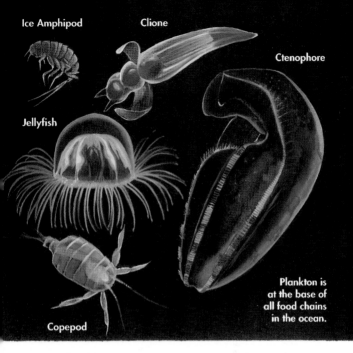

Ice Amphipod

Clione

Ctenophore

Jellyfish

Copepod

Plankton is at the base of all food chains in the ocean.

serve as food for other animals in the food chains of the sea.

Already there are strong indications that the plankton pastures of the open ocean are being affected by pollutants washed in from the land. These small life forms are not on threatened or endangered species lists, and most people would consider it strange even to think in those terms. But if the abundance of plankton was sharply reduced, all life on earth would be imperiled. The web of life is complex, and the oceans are vital to sustaining life. At present the harmful effects of pollution in the seas are most noticeable in coastal areas, but there are many indications that pollutants are affecting ocean life on a broad scale.

Great Auk

GREAT AUKS were penguinlike flightless birds that stood about 2 feet tall. They once existed by the millions in the North Atlantic. On the land a Great Auk waddled on its big webbed feet and used its short, flipperlike wings to help it keep its balance. In the water it could swim swiftly, dive deep, and stay under for long periods of time.

Bones found along the shores of northern seas are evidence that early Europeans ate the Great Auk and burned its fat as fuel. The Great Auk had become extinct and had been long forgotten in northern Europe for many centuries when it was rediscovered by explorers in the New World. There the killing began again, the Great Auk becoming a staple in the diets of anglers working the northern seas.

Adult birds were clubbed to death. Birds not eaten right away were salted and put in barrels for storage aboard ships that took them to Europe. The Great Auks' eggs were considered by many to be a special delicacy, and the feathers were saved for stuffing mattresses and pillows. Harvesting time was usually in summer, when large groups of birds came to shore to nest. The birds were driven into pens for slaughter.

By around 1750, the Great Auk had become too scarce to make commercial harvesting practical. The killing was continued on a smaller scale. When it was obvious that the Great Auk was becoming extinct, museums commissioned hunters to get skins for mounting and to be used for displays in specimen cases. On Eldey Island off Iceland, a few dozen birds came ashore every season to nest. The hunters found them, and in a short time the very last Great Auk was dead and on its way to a British museum. If the museum curators had been less concerned about getting specimens, the Great Auk might have survived.

LABRADOR DUCKS lived along the Atlantic coast of North America and apparently nested along the Gulf of St. Lawrence. They traveled as far south as Chesapeake Bay in winter. Handsome little ducks, the males were bluish black with white wing patches and white on the head and neck. Females were brownish.

Never abundant, the Labrador Duck was found in shallow coastal waters, where it fed on shellfish. Some scientists think its decline was due to hunting plus a rapid increase in human populations, which caused shellfish populations to decrease.

The most rapid decline occurred between 1850 and 1870, and the last of the Labrador Ducks was shot about 1875. Without hunting, this little duck might have survived, but

Labrador Duck

the evidence does indicate that it was becoming extinct even before humans arrived on the scene.

SEA MINK were the Atlantic Ocean's equivalent of the Sea Otters in the Pacific. They lived on rocks in the coastal waters from Newfoundland to Massachusetts, with the greatest concentration apparently along the coast of Maine.

Twice as large as mink living along inland waters, the Sea Mink had thick reddish fur. Its pelt brought a high price. By 1880 the Sea Mink was extinct. Oddly, its identification as a species came posthumously, more than a quarter of a century after the animal itself was no longer in existence.

Sea Mink

GREEN TURTLES got their name from the bluish green color of their fat, prized for making a clear-broth soup. Grazing on turtle grass in the warm shallows of the Caribbean gave their flesh an appealing veal-like flavor.

Green Turtles were once so abundant in the Caribbean and elsewhere that they were compared to the American Bison on the Great Plains. Millions were harvested. Their nests were destroyed and robbed of their eggs by people, dogs, pigs, and wild animals. New hatchlings running for water from their sandy nests were easy prey.

Like the American Bison's, the Green Turtle's population began to diminish—so rapidly, in fact, that it was feared the turtles would soon disappear altogether. An international organization was formed to aid the Green Turtle, and a hatchery was established that released baby turtles into the sea. It now appears that the Green Turtle will be spared.

Other endangered sea turtles include the Atlantic Ridley, the Hawksbill, and the giant Leatherback. The Loggerhead is no longer abundant but so far is not on the endangered list.

Green Turtle

102

Brown Pelicans

BROWN PELICANS, until recently, were in a serious decline. Yet these big birds were not hunted, either for food or for their feathers. Occasionally a fisherman might become annoyed by a Brown Pelican competing for a fish. But typically the bird eats only so-called trash fish, which have little or no value to sport or commercial anglers.

What killed large numbers of Brown Pelicans? It was DDT picked up from the fish they ate. The small dose a bird got from each fish built up in the bird's body—a process called *biological magnification*. DDT breaks down into a chemical compound called DDE, which adversely affects calcium metabolism. Eggs laid by females that ingested DDE were thin-shelled and broke before hatching. This continued year after year until the Brown Pelican's population slumped to a low from which recovery seemed unlikely. But happily, the ban on the use of DDT since 1972 has made recovery possible. The Brown Pelican is becoming abundant again. The major hazard to the birds today is entanglement in the hooks, lines, and nets of fishermen.

SHORT-TAILED (OR STELLER'S) ALBATROSSES were once abundant across the Pacific Ocean. The wings of these giants among birds spanned some 7 feet. Large numbers nesting on islands along the coast of Asia became victims of hunters who killed the birds to get their feathers. The largest nesting colony was on Torishima, a volcanic island about 400 miles south of Tokyo. Eruptions of the volcano, in 1939 and then again in 1941, destroyed almost all of the remaining birds. In 1957 the Japanese government made the island into a reserve, hoping to bring the birds back. No one really knows exactly how many are alive today, but one estimate is less than 200.

SEA OTTERS, the smallest of all marine mammals, are carnivores that inhabit the Pacific Ocean, where they were discovered in 1741 by that same Russian expedition that also found Steller's Sea Cow (see p. 138). Reaching 5 feet in length and weighing as much as 80 pounds, they are stockier in build than the more weasel-like otters that live in fresh waters. The Sea Otter eats, mates, and even sleeps in water, usually no more than half a mile offshore in a bed of kelp. At night it wraps some strands of kelp around its body to keep from drifting into the open ocean.

The Sea Otter's diet consists of sea urchins and some fish and shellfish. After a food-collecting dive, the Sea Otter surfaces and floats on its back to eat. Some shellfish can be opened easily by the Sea Otter's teeth. For those shellfish with thicker shells, the Sea Otter finds a flat stone, puts it on its chest, then pounds the shell against the stone to crack it. Sea Otters also use stones as hammers to knock abalones loose from rocks.

Soon after they were discovered by the Russians, Sea Otters began to be pursued for their thick, glossy pelts. The trade lasted for about a century and a half, but most of the Sea Otters were gone within the first hundred years. By the late 1800s they were rare, and by 1918 they were thought to be extinct. But just in case some might be left, the United States, Russia, Great Britain, and Japan signed an agreement at that time making it illegal to hunt Sea Otters.

Twenty years passed before any Sea Otters were seen again. Then two breeding colonies were discovered. Given full protection, Sea Otters now number more than 100,000. But they are still threatened, this time by commercial oil from spills, which destroys the insulating properties of their hair.

Sea Otter

Southern Fur Seal

SEALS once lived in colonies of up to a million animals. The Southern Fur Seal lived and thrived along the southern coast of California south to Mexico. Prized for its fur, however, it was slaughtered in countless numbers and was believed to have become extinct. In 1954 a few animals were discovered on the rocky island of Guadalupe off Baja California. This protected population is now building slowly.

Earless seals have bristly hair rather than short, soft underfur, but this did not spare them from being hunted for oil, meat, and hides. Most abundant (and not endangered) today is the Crabeater Seal of the remote Antarctic, its population estimated to be approximately 15 to 40 million. Its numbers have actually increased since its main food source, krill, has become more abundant due to the slaughter of Antarctic baleen whales.

Almost all of the animals in this group, which includes walruses and sea lions, have been pursued by hide hunters, spared only when it became no longer profitable to harvest them. International laws can prevent their extinction, but not all nations have agreed to abide by such regulations.

DOLPHINS and porpoises, smaller cousins of the big whales, are commonly trapped and die in the nets of commercial fishermen. So many are killed each year in this manner that the dolphin and porpoise populations are declining. Pressure has been exerted recently to force commercial fishermen to use nets that do not entangle the animals, and so the future for at least some species seems somewhat brighter than it did thirty years ago.

Bottlenose Dolphins

Blue Whale

BLUE WHALES, the largest animals to have ever lived, can measure more than 100 feet long and weigh as much as 175 tons. Yet they subsist on a diet of plankton and tiny shrimplike krill.

Blue Whales gorge on food in Antarctic or Arctic waters during the summer months. In a day's time a giant whale may draw in as much as 4 tons of krill, and it may add 20 tons or more to its weight during the months of feeding. When winter comes to the Antarctic, the big whales travel northward to warmer waters. During these months the whales mate but do not feed, surviving on the blubber built up during the feeding season.

Only a few thousand Blue Whales exist today, their numbers reduced by commercial whaling from an estimated 250,000. Like other whales—nearly all of which are threatened—they are protected by international agreements. But not all countries abide by the regulations. Further, some of these regulations seem to benefit whalers more than whales.

Whales, dolphins, and porpoises have captured the public's attention more than most other groups of animals, and support programs are helping. A few species of whales are increasing in numbers, among them California's Gray Whale, which in 1994 became the first marine mammal to be taken off the Endangered Species list.

MANATEES inhabit warm seas, estuaries, and rivers. They have thick, spindle-shaped bodies with solid, heavy bones. Although they have no hind legs or flippers, their paddlelike front legs and broad, flat tails supply the power for swimming. The manatee's round head, small, piglike eyes, and large, flexible lips with bristles above give the animal a strange appearance. Nevertheless, these big mammals are thought to have contributed strongly to the mermaid myth.

Strictly plant eaters, manatees are also called sea cows,

and many people found them tasty fare. The giant Steller's Sea Cow (see p. 138) was eaten into extinction within 50 years of its discovery.

The closely related Dugong of the Indian Ocean is also endangered, as are all three remaining species of manatees—the West African, Amazon, and West Indian. Those that have escaped slaughter find survival difficult today because of the loss of their habitats and also because of injuries inflicted on them by the propellers of boats.

West Indian Manatees

ISLANDS

There are two basic island types: continental and oceanic. Continental islands are close to major landmasses, and they share with them the same kinds of soil, rocks, animals, and plants. Oceanic islands, in contrast, are far from major landmasses. Some are volcanic in origin; others are formed of coral. Because they are remote, their plant and animal life is usually distinctive.

Animals reached their oceanic island homes originally by flying, swimming, or floating. Winds and stormy seas have been responsible for the introduction of some species. In recent times many animals and plants have been taken to islands by human settlers.

The original inhabitants of oceanic islands may remain isolated for so many generations that they lose all but the most superficial resemblance to their mainland relatives. Darwin's Finches of the Galápagos Islands, for example, differ greatly from the finches on the mainland. Some have extremely long, slim bills for sipping nectar from deep-throated flowers; others have heavy bills for probing into bark and holes in wood for insects and their larvae; still others have sharp hawklike bills and are predators. These and other such specializations equipped Darwin's Finches for occupying island niches that on the mainland are inhabited by birds belonging to entirely different families.

Remoteness from competitors once provided protection for most island dwellers. But the appearance of humans on the islands destroyed this isolation. Even if people do not try to eliminate the native species directly, introduced domestic or wild animals may take over their food and living space or prey on the island dwellers. Some of the most tragic examples of human-caused extinction have occurred on oceanic islands.

DELALANDE'S COUCALS lived in the wet forests along the northeastern coast of Madagascar. Coucals are ground-nesting members of the cuckoo family. Delalande's Coucals survived until about the year 1930, then became extinct as their habitat was destroyed.

Other Madagascan birds teetering on the brink of extinction are the Thick-billed Cuckoo, Soumagne's Owl, the Madagascar Teal, and the Long-tailed Ground Roller. All are victims of habitat destruction.

Delalande's Coucal

DODOES were pigeons the size of turkeys. They lived on the island of Mauritius, which is approximately 600 miles east of the island of Madagascar in the Indian Ocean, and had no natural enemies. Then Dutch explorers arrived in 1598. The big flightless birds were easily killed with clubs and eaten.

Mauritius became a regular stop for sailing vessels, their purpose: to stock their larders with Dodoes. Monkeys and pigs brought to the island by European settlers ate the Dodoes' eggs and destroyed their nests. Dodo Birds became extinct in less than a hundred years, leaving behind only the familiar expression "as dead as a Dodo."

Had the Dodo lived, it might have been domesticated and become an important staple in our diet, like chickens, turkeys, and ducks. Or, the Dodo might have contributed to producing a superior hybrid fowl. We will never know.

Dodo

113

Elephant Bird

ELEPHANT BIRDS once lived on Madagascar. They were giants—up to 10 feet tall and about half a ton in weight. The females laid 50-pound eggs. Natural changes in its habitat and the taking of eggs by natives probably caused the demise of this behemoth, believed to have inspired the legendary Roc, told of by Sinbad the Sailor in the Arabian classic tale *The Thousand and One Nights*.

HAWAIIAN HONEYCREEPERS were members of a family of almost 30 species of birds. A third of these are now extinct and the rest are critically endangered. Similar to Darwin's Finches of the Galápagos Islands, honeycreepers became adapted to every available niche. Most had long, narrow bills used for sipping nectar from flowers, but some had short, thick bills for cracking open seeds, sharp bills for catching insect prey, or stout bills for drilling into tree trunks, like woodpeckers.

What caused them to become extinct? Some were victims of habitat destruction. Others could not compete with introduced birds or were preyed upon by introduced mammals. Still others were killed by diseases brought to the Hawaiian islands.

Among the extinct is the Mamo, a nectar feeder that was prized for its handsome, glossy black feathers, which were used to make cloaks for the Hawaiian royalty. Continued hunting for feathers by some white settlers also contributed to the bird's annihilation, as did the cutting down of the forests where it lived. Evidence shows that the last of the Mamos apparently died before 1900.

Hawaiian Honeycreeper

MOAS were wingless birds of New Zealand, similar to the Elephant Bird of Madagascar. Some of the 13 or so species were no bigger than domestic chickens, but others stood up to 12 feet tall. A few are believed to have survived to nearly 1800, but no European ever saw one alive. They were hunted for food and driven to extinction by the native Maoris.

Moa

MAURITIUS KESTRELS are nearly extinct. These birds nested in trees on Mauritius. When the island was settled, nearly all the trees were cut down, and monkeys introduced to the island robbed the nests of the few remaining birds. Also, the birds had fed mainly on lizards, but when shrubs were added to the island's vegetation, the lizards were able to hide from the birds.

The Mauritius Kestrel became the last survivor of more than a dozen native island birds that were victims mainly of habitat destruction.

Mauritius Kestrel

115

Tuatara

TUATARAS, or Sphenodons, are literally "living fossils," for they are the only descendants left of a group of animals that lived on earth some 200 million years ago. The most primitive of all reptiles, a Tuatara looks much like a thick-bodied lizard. Also like a lizard, it has a unique third "eye" hidden in the middle of its head. This "eye" has a transparent covering and presumably functions well enough in the youthful Tuatara for it to distinguish light from dark.

At one time these unusual reptiles were found all over New Zealand. Now the few thousand remaining Tuataras are confined to the dozen or so small islands in the strait between New Zealand's two main islands. Some think they were destroyed on the mainland by introduced rats. They are currently protected by law.

116

KOMODO DRAGONS are the world's largest lizards, measuring 8 feet long or even longer and weighing as much as 300 pounds. These huge lizards eat mainly wild pigs and deer but will also feed on smaller animals and carrion.

Preserves were set up on the island of Komodo in 1926 to prevent the extinction of Komodo Dragons due to loss of habitat. But the law has not always been able to guarantee the safety of the several thousand animals that are left, since they still have to compete with people for food. Because of their limited distribution, they could become extinct were there to be a natural or other disaster affecting the four islands on which they are found.

A few Komodo Dragons have been exhibited in zoos, where some have been bred successfully. But there is still much to be done to save these amazing Indonesian lizards.

Komodo Dragon

GALÁPAGOS TORTOISES, some of which may weigh as much as 500 pounds, once basked by the hundreds of thousands on the rocky Galápagos Islands off the northwestern coast of South America. In fact, *galápagos* is the Spanish word for "tortoise."

Explorers and whalers soon discovered that the tortoises were good to eat. Important in the days before refrigeration, too, the big tortoises could be kept alive in a ship's hold for weeks without needing either food or water. They provided a steady supply of fresh meat.

In addition to huge numbers of Galápagos Tortoises that

were hauled off the islands for food, the dogs, rats, and pigs introduced to the islands ate the young tortoises as well as destroyed nests and eggs. Ecuador finally passed protective laws to spare the species from extinction, and today several thousand tortoises again bask on the islands.

Galápagos Tortoises

Also endangered on the islands, due primarily to habitat destruction, are native penguins, hawks, and cormorants. Ecuador is working with conservationists to restore the populations of these unique birds and other island animals. However, undoing centuries of harm is difficult, particularly where there is continued competition with people for space.

Kiwi

KIWIS must certainly rank
among the most unusual of
all birds. Plump, chickenlike,
and unable to fly, they have
come to symbolize their native home of New Zealand. Kiwis
live in burrows and do most of their feeding at night,
hunting for worms and other small crawling creatures. Their
eyesight is poor, but nostrils that open at the tip of their long
bill give them a keen sense of smell. Bristles at the base of
the bill serve as antennae, or feelers. Kiwi hens lay eggs that
weigh about a fourth of their own body weight. At one time
heavily hunted and preyed upon by introduced mammals,
Kiwis are no longer common. Now protected by law, they
may escape annihilation.

CAHOWS are petrels that once lived on the Caribbean
island of Bermuda. Their existence was peaceful until the
1500s, when the early British settlers brought pigs over to
the island. The pigs destroyed the nests and eggs of the
Cahow. During a famine in the early 1600s, the settlers
themselves ate the birds. Later, rats that had arrived with the
settlers attacked the young birds and destroyed their nests.
The Cahow appeared to be extinct. Three centuries passed.

Then, in the early 1950s, a few Cahows were spotted on rocky offshore islands. Here they were free of people, pigs, and rats, but they now had a new problem. They could not dig nesting burrows in the rocks, so they began to make their nests in rocky crevices. But when White-tailed Tropic Birds arrived on the islands, they invaded the crevices and killed the Cahow chicks.

This time people came to their rescue. They carved artificial entrances in the crevices big enough for the Cahows but too small for the White-tailed Tropic Birds. The Cahow accepted them and began increasing in numbers. Then suddenly their eggs stopped hatching. The reason? DDT poisoning, the same problem that has affected the Brown Pelican, Bald Eagle, and other birds. With the use of these pesticides now banned, it is hoped that the Cahow will make a second comeback.

Cahows

NENE, or Hawaiian Geese, are medium-sized fawn, brown, and black geese that were once a popular food for people. For about a month every year while it molts, the bird cannot fly; during this time it is easily killed with clubs. Nest disturbances by humans and certain ranching developments, such as allowing cows and goats to destroy edible native vegetation, also added to the Nene's decline. Introduced predators such as cats, mongooses, dogs, rats, and pigs also took their toll, eating young birds and destroying nests and eggs. By about 1900 the great flocks were gone, and only a few birds were left in the wild.

One man recognized the bird's steadily worsening plight and built up a flock of 42 birds. This flock was destroyed by a tsunami in 1946, but a few birds that had escaped the pens earlier managed to survive this disaster. The government then began working to save the birds. Preserves were set aside on the islands of Hawaii and Maui, and an intensive breeding program was begun. Some birds have even been released into the wild. The Nene is making a comeback and in fact has become Hawaii's official state bird.

Nene

Monkey-eating
Eagle

MONKEY-EATING EAGLES now live only on the island of
Mindanao in the Philippines. Fewer than 50 of these very
large eagles are alive today. They are 3 feet long, from
beak to tail, and their plumage consists of big patches of
white, reddish brown, and black feathers. Their most
distinctive feature is their unkempt, frazzled crest. These
huge predators do indeed eat monkeys, but they also prey
on other sizable mammals and birds. In turn, they have
been hunted by the natives. Although they have been exhibited in zoos, they have so far not bred in captivity.

Loss of their forest habitat is the major reason for their
decline. The taking of Monkey-eating Eagles for trophies
and zoos may have further reduced their population to its
critical low. The birds' boldness in attacking dogs near
dwellings or going after domestic fowl or livestock has not
endeared them to natives, either. This is not unusual, of
course. Nowhere in the world are large predators safe from
the humans who compete with them for food.

Takahe

Kagu

TAKAHES are flightless birds the size of turkeys. They live in New Zealand and have bright greenish-blue plumage and a red bill. Competition with introduced deer led to their decline. Takahes were thought to have become extinct before 1900, but in 1948 about a hundred birds were discovered in a remote valley. Protected by the government in a national park, they have continued to increase in number until now there are several thousand.

KAGUS are birds that live on the forest floor in New Caledonia. They were formerly widespread, but after the arrival of white settlers who hunted them primarily for their plumes, the birds fled to the deep forests and the mountains. But even there they could not escape attacks by dogs, cats, and other introduced predators. As a result of these factors, the unusual and distinctively plumed Kagus are now threatened with extinction, even though a preserve has been established for them on the island.

TASMANIAN WOLVES, or Thylacines, are collie-sized carnivorous marsupial mammals confined to Tasmania, an island off the southeastern coast of Australia. Ranchers on the island complained that Tasmanian Wolves preyed on their sheep and other livestock, and so the government offered bounties for any that were killed. When the animals disappeared from sight entirely, a large preserve was set aside for them, but so far there have been no occupants.

TASMANIAN DEVILS are badger-sized pouch-bearing marsupials originally found in Australia. Like Tasmanian Wolves, they were forced into making a final stand in Tasmania. Here they appear to be surviving. A Tasmanian Devil looks like a small bear, its coat jet black with a few patches of white. Stockily built, the Tasmanian Devil can be quite fierce-looking and give off loud, devilish growls. Its ferocity, however, has been exaggerated, as it fights mainly with its own kind over food.

Tasmanian Wolf

Tasmanian Devil

SOLENODONS are shrewlike nocturnal mammals that measure about 12 inches long, with a naked tail almost equally long. Two species inhabit Cuba and other islands in the Caribbean. Both are rare, and if their forest reserves are not managed properly, they may follow the West Indian shrews that declined to extinction upon the arrival of the Europeans. Factors contributing to their demise are habitat destruction, a low rate of reproduction (they usually have no more than three, and more often only one, young per litter), and introduced predators such as cats, dogs, and mongooses.

HUTIAS are squirrel-sized rodents that are found in the Caribbean. Excluding bats, the Jamaican Hutia is the only native mammal still living in Jamaica. A related species lives on a coral island in the Bahamas, and two others are found in the Dominican Republic and Haiti. All are endangered, due to habitat destruction, predation by the introduced mongoose, and their being hunted for food. Also, hutias have a very low reproductive rate. Females rarely produce litters of more than one or two young, and the gestation period is very long.

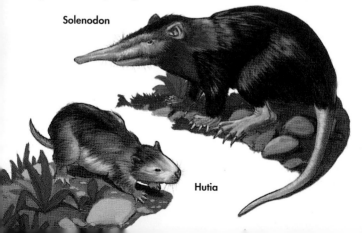

Solenodon

Hutia

Javan Rhinoceros

RHINOCEROSES on the islands of Sumatra and Java are endangered, as are the Black and the White Rhinos that live on the African savannas. Both the Sumatran and the Javan Rhinos once lived on the continents, too, but they were hunted into extinction there. Rhinos are usually killed for their horns, which are pulverized and then sold for their supposed magical and medicinal powers. Even some of the animals now living in sanctuaries have become victims of poachers who kill the animals, cut off their horns, and leave the carcasses to rot.

A Sumatran Rhino stands about 4½ feet tall at the shoulders and weighs about 1 ton. It is the smallest of the living rhinos. Both sexes have two horns, the female's smaller than the male's. Compared to that of other rhinos, the skin is smoother and has fewer folds. Only about 800 to 1,000 Sumatran Rhinos are believed to exist today.

The Javan Rhino stands about 5½ feet tall at the shoulders. Males have one horn, females usually none. The skin is thick, with the neck and shoulder folds prominent. Fewer than two dozen are alive today.

127

Lowland Anoa

ANOAS are small wild cattle that live in Indonesia. They are extremely rare, due to hunting, destruction of their habitat, and diseases picked up from domestic livestock. Survivors have retreated into very remote areas. One subspecies stands only slightly more than 2 feet tall at the shoulders. The largest is about 3 feet tall. Anoas have thick, nearly hairless hides, and their horns are more than a foot long.

KEY DEER stand about 2½ feet tall at the shoulders. This smallest American deer is a subspecies of the larger White-tailed Deer, which is found on the mainland. Key Deer are found only in the Florida Keys. As a result of hunting, natural disasters, and the destruction of their habitat by developers, there were only about 30 Key Deer left in 1950. At that time, a 7,000-acre refuge was set up for the animals

Key Deer

on Big Pine Key. Here they have increased in number but are still endangered, their biggest threat now being cars speeding along the Overseas Highway. But basically this is another turnaround story of which we need more.

TAMARAW are wild cattle that live in bamboo thickets high on the mountain slopes of Mindoro Island in the Philippines. Only a few hundred of these animals are left. Hunting them is illegal, but the law is not enforced. Some of the kills are made from airplanes and helicopters.

Only 3½ feet tall at the shoulders, Tamaraw are grayish black with short, thick horns that slant backward. These rather gentle animals once grazed in the daytime, out in the open, but now they graze at night.

Tamaraw

AYE-AYES are found only on the island of Madagascar, about 250 miles east of Mozambique in southeastern Africa. Only a few thousand are believed to be alive today.

Although at first classified as a rodent, the cat-sized Aye-aye is a primitive primate. Nocturnal and solitary, it has a long, bushy tail and thick grayish fur. Its eyes are owlish, its ears are large and rounded, and its hind legs are much longer than its front legs. Most unusual are its slim, bony fingers. The especially long third finger is used to probe for insect larvae in holes in wood and to scoop out the edible, pithy cores of coconuts, sugarcane, and other plant stems.

The animal's steady decline in the wild is due mainly to the destruction of its forest habitat. Some natives consider it sacred and do not bother it, but others consider it a bad omen and shoot it on sight.

Aye-aye

Indri

INDRIS are monkeylike primitive primates that live in the forests of Madagascar. Standing more than 3 feet tall, they are the largest of the present-day lemurs. Compared to the size of their body, their head is small and their tail is reduced to a stump. Their big toe is sufficiently separated from the other four toes so that they have a firm grip.

Indris are mostly black, with broad patches of white on the arms, rump, and head and neck. They live high in the trees of the rainforest. When they do come to the ground, they walk erect on their hind legs. They look so humanlike that the natives once believed they were dwarfs that had gone into the forests to live. They have powerful voices, emitting loud, doglike howls.

Indris are rare in captivity. Their numbers in the wild have declined to a dangerous low, mainly because of the deforestation of Madagascar. Their survival is not likely.

131

Fork-marked
Mouse
Lemur

Sifaka

Mongoose
Lemur

Gray Gentle Lemur

132

SIFAKAS are primitive primates that live on the island of Madagascar. Their body is covered with white fur, but their naked, or hairless, face is black and looks like a mask. Like the Indris, they were very common up to the 1930s, but all of the several kinds remaining are now in danger because of the destruction of their forest habitat.

LEMURS are also primitive primates. All are endangered because of the cutting of the forests and the taking over of land by people. Mongoose Lemurs, slightly smaller than cats, were never common. The few remaining inhabit the Comoro Islands and northwestern Madagascar.

The Fork-marked Mouse Lemur is less than 12 inches long. The "fork-marked" part of its name comes from the black stripe that extends from its rump to the crown of its head, where it divides, or "forks." The tail is longer than the body and is bushy. The Fork-marked Mouse Lemur spends its days sleeping in the hollows of trees, sometimes sharing its home with bees and eating some of the honey.

One subspecies of the Gray Gentle Lemur is found only in the reed beds around Lake Alaotra. About 1½ feet long with an equally long tail, this swimming lemur has serrated teeth used for chewing bamboo and other fibrous stems.

The Fat-tailed Dwarf Lemur's thick tail acts as a reserve of food energy when the animal becomes dormant during the hot, dry season. This lemur has a broad, catlike face, and its eyes have dark rings.

Fat-tailed
Dwarf Lemur

Sulawesi Macaque

SULAWESI MACAQUES are found on Sulawesi, a group of islands between Borneo and New Guinea. They are also known as Black Apes. Although they are macaques, their faces are longer than those of other species. They have a tufted crown and only a stub of a tail. They are now endangered as a result of a loss of habitat and also because they are hunted for meat or as agricultural pests.

ORANGUTANS, which live in the jungles of Borneo and Sumatra, are the only great apes found outside Africa. Males may stand 4½ feet tall and weigh about 200 pounds. Females are at least a third smaller. Orangutans have exceptionally long arms, which they use to swing from branch to branch. On the ground they clench their fists and use their arms like crutches to push themselves along. There are two subspecies of Orangutans, the Borneans and the Sumatrans.

134

Orangutan is a Malayan word that means "man of the woods." These intelligent primates are indeed humanlike in both looks and manner. In captivity they are very extroverted and easy to breed. But because the island forests where they are found are rapidly being destroyed and because until recently they were collected for the pet trade in the Far East, Orangutans are still among the most endangered of all animals. Only about 40,000 are believed to exist today.

Orangutan

MOUNTAIN PEAKS AND POLAR REGIONS

The peaks of the earth's highest mountains are perpetually capped with snow. Conditions there are almost identical with those in the polar regions. Below these caps are treeless regions similar to the tundra, and still farther down are wide bands of coniferous trees, then deciduous trees, and finally, in some cases, tropical forests. The highest mountains in the equatorial regions contain all of these zones.

On the world's highest mountains, life is limited not only by the cold but also by the much lower atmospheric pressure and greatly reduced amount of oxygen. Yet some birds and mammals are never found at elevations of much less than 10,000 feet. Other animals go into the mountains in the summer, then move back to the warmer lowlands in the winter. For a few threatened species, the mountains have become their last refuge on earth.

No single, distinctive landmass defines the Arctic. Rather, the north polar region consists of a sea of ice that is no more than a few feet thick in some places and more than a hundred feet thick in other places. The Arctic seas are constantly cold. They lack the benefit of the warm currents that stir in nutrients and enrich Antarctic waters. Thus, life is not abundant in Arctic waters.

The land surrounding the North Pole is a vast treeless tundra carpeted with snow from six to nine months of the year. Tundra lands are permanently frozen—to almost half a mile deep in some places. In summer the top few inches thaw, and the tundra then briefly burgeons with life. The previously barren land rapidly turns first green and then multicolored, with flowers in bloom. The sun shines around the clock at the peak of summer. Since the growing season is brief, no time is lost in producing seeds or other fruiting bodies. During this period, too, the tundra becomes crowded with animal life.

Penguins can still be spotted on Antarctic shores, but there are fewer today than ever before.

Antarctica, the last continent to be discovered and explored, is an immense expanse of ice and snow that lies on the South Pole. Separated from all other lands and beyond the frigid southern extensions of the Indian, Pacific, and Atlantic oceans, it is essentially uninhabitable. Its waters were first explored by hunters pursuing migrating seals and whales. The interior of Antarctica is a virtual desert—cold, stormy, and windswept. Humans are the only living things to have probed the icy interior of this great continent.

Unlike the desolate interior, however, the coastal waters, surrounding seas, and nearby islands are astonishingly rich with life as a result of the convergence of several warm and cold currents. Plankton is abundant in summer. Penguins and other seabirds, plus whales, dolphins, and seals, are found in the coastal waters and along the shores. The remoteness and hostility of the Antarctic have thus far spared these animals from total annihilation, but many are listed among threatened species.

Spectacled Cormorant

SPECTACLED CORMORANTS are known today mostly from museum specimens. Poor flyers, they lived on islands in the Bering Sea. The bare areas surrounding their eyes, which looked a little like spectacles, gave them their name. Visitors to the islands clubbed the big seabirds to death and ate them. The last of the Spectacled Cormorants were killed in the mid-1800s.

STELLER'S SEA COW was up to 20 feet long and weighed almost 4 tons. Related to the smaller manatees and the Dugong, which live in tropical waters, Steller's Sea Cows inhabited islands in the Bering Sea. They were first seen in 1741 during a Russian expedition and were named for the German naturalist and chief scientist of the expedition, Georg Steller. Forced to winter on the islands after their ship was wrecked, members of the expedition tried eating various fish, birds, and mammals and liked the huge, wrinkly Steller's Sea Cows best of all.

The explorers, whalers, and seal hunters who visited the region in the following years also ate the big sea cows. The total original population was probably less than 2,000 animals, and by 1770 no Steller's Sea Cows were still alive.

Steller's Sea Cow

California Condor

CONDORS are the largest of the world's vultures, and both the California Condor and Andean Condor are in danger of extinction. Fewer than 1,000 Andeans are left in the wild, and the only known living California Condors, fewer than 70 of them, are in zoos in San Diego and Los Angeles. It is hoped that the offspring of these birds can eventually be released into the wild. Without human help, neither condor is expected to survive much past the year 2000.

Both condors have wingspans of about 9½ feet, with the Andean Condor's very slightly the larger of the two. Neither is prolific. A female condor lays only one egg every other year. The young bird is completely helpless for more than six months, then continues to stay with its mother for an additional six months.

Condors have been in existence since the days of the mastodons and saber-toothed tigers. At that time, the California Condor ranged over most of the West and, in smaller numbers, east of the Rockies. Since about 1900, however, it has been confined to southwestern California.

Like all vultures, condors are scavengers. As the land became settled, the carcasses of large wild animals and nesting sites became scarce. The big birds also became targets of "sport" shooters.

139

Trumpeter Swan

TRUMPETER SWANS once lived over much of the northern United States and Canada, but by about 1900 they were believed to be extinct. Then a dozen or so survivors were found in Yellowstone National Park, where they were given strict protection. Today several thousand of these birds live in Yellowstone and in other parks in the United States and Canada.

CHINCHILLAS are
squirrel-sized rodents
that live in the Andes.
Long prized for their
luxurious, silky fur made
into coats and capes, they
are now raised on farms. But wild
chinchillas are still hunted because their fur is richer. Also,
gestation for these animals is long, and a female produces
only one to two litters per year. Some experts fear that wild
chinchillas will soon become extinct. Some farm-raised chinchillas might eventually be released into the wild to help
replenish the stock of wild animals.

VOLCANO RABBITS live on the high slopes in south-central
Mexico. They have short ears and no tail. They communicate with each other by giving high-pitched squeals. These
interesting and unusual rabbits are disappearing because of
the destruction of the pine forests and the grasslands where
they live. They are also heavily hunted by people from
nearby Mexico City.

Volcano Rabbits

141

POLAR BEARS, their numbers now stable at about 20,000, have been hunted almost wholly for sport—to see who could bag the biggest or get some portion of the animal to exhibit as a trophy. In days gone by, Polar Bear hunting did indeed require both endurance and skill. First came a long voyage by ship through Arctic waters and then a trip by dogsled. The hunter, when finally coming face-to-face with the half-ton animal, knew that the big bear could easily tear him to pieces unless he felled it with his first shot.

In the 1940s hunters began using much more powerful and rapid-firing weapons and did most of their hunting from either an airplane or a helicopter. When a bear was sighted, the pilot landed and the hunter got in position, usually under a white cover so that the bear did not even suspect his presence. Then the pilot took off again and flew low over the bear to herd it in the hunter's direction, using a radio all the while to communicate with the hunter.

Today only natives are allowed to kill the Polar Bear, and only for food or hides. About 1,000 are taken each year. However, the Polar Bear's existence in the wild may be seriously threatened by the exploitation of Arctic oil and gas reserves in the limited areas suitable for denning by pregnant females. Many zoos have Polar Bears on exhibit. Fortunately, they do well in captivity and produce young.

SPECTACLED BEARS live high in the mountains of South America, at elevations of from 1,000 to 14,000 feet. They get their name from the yellowish-white marks circling their eyes. Since they are now very rare, their survival may well rest with those several dozen in zoos, where, like other bears, they adapt well and produce young. These medium-sized bears are almost exclusively vegetarian, but they have been hunted for sport, for meat, for their skins, and because some ranchers consider them a threat to livestock, which they are not.

Polar Bears

Spectacled Bear

143

GRIZZLY BEARS are huge, hump-shouldered Brown Bears, with long guard hairs in their coat that are lighter in color at the tips, thus giving the bears a grizzled or silvery appearance. Males may stand 8 feet tall and weigh nearly half a ton. Females are a third smaller than the males. Both reach their peak weight in late summer or fall, when they become well fattened for their winter sleep. Hibernation periods for Grizzlies can vary, starting between the months of October and December and ending somewhere between March and May. Exact dates depend on factors such as location, weather, and health of the bear.

Despite its formidable size and long, curved front claws, a Grizzly Bear's normal diet in the wild is 90 percent fruit, nuts, roots, and green vegetation. The remainder consists of some live prey, plus carrion. Grizzlies are opportunists. When salmon are running and relatively easy to catch, the bears gorge on fresh-caught fish. They will also eat insects, mice, marmots, deer, or whatever else is available and easily caught. They will even raid garbage cans in parks and in towns, and this puts them in conflict with people.

In the early nineteenth century, there may have been up to 100,000 Grizzly Bears roaming over most of North America west of the Rocky Mountains from Mexico to Alaska. Their population has now dwindled to probably under 1,000. Those remaining are found only in wilderness areas. A few live in Yellowstone National Park.

The Grizzly Bear has always been a prime quarry itself, killed for its meat and hide and also because people felt it was too large and potentially too dangerous to have near settlements. Ranchers have also considered it a threat to their livestock. In their natural setting these big bears have no match for size, but the combined effects of guns, dogs, traps, and poisons, as well as the continued shrinking of the wilderness areas in which they live, have brought them to their present state of near annihilation.

GIANT PANDAS, once thought to belong to the same family as raccoons, are now believed to be more closely related to bears. Often weighing more than 300 pounds and attaining a height of 5 feet, Giant Pandas eat almost exclusively the shoots and tender young branches of bamboo. Long ago they roamed across eastern Asia, but then their habitat shrank to only mountain locales. Europeans did not know of them until 1869, when they were seen and described by Père David, a French missionary.

The first Giant Panda to reach the West was exhibited in a Chicago zoo in 1937. By 1941 eight additional animals were in U.S. zoos and more were soon on exhibit in Europe. Pandas do not breed easily in captivity, however. And loss of habitat plus being hunted for their thick, woolly pelts have caused their further decline in the wild.

Eventually, the government of China placed the pandas under strict protection. The remaining animals—perhaps fewer than 1,000 of them—live in Central China, in bamboo forests at elevations of 5,000 to 10,000 feet.

ANDEAN CATS, which live high in the Andes of South America, prey on viscachas and other rodents. No one really knows how many still exist, but they are apparently extremely rare. Geoffroy's Cat, which at about 3 feet long is slightly smaller than the Andean Cat, lives at lower elevations. Its numbers have dwindled, too, as has the number of existing Kodkods, or Chilean Mountain Cats. All three must be watched to assure their survival.

Andean Cat

Giant Panda

Spanish Lynx

SPANISH LYNXES live in the mountains of southern Spain. Only a few thousand are left, a remnant population of the European Lynx that once roamed over most of Europe.

The Spanish Lynx is slightly smaller and has shorter fur than the lynxes that still live in limited numbers in the "North Woods" of North America and also in northern Europe and Asia. It also has a short tail and prominent ear tufts. Like other predators at the top of the food pyramid, it needs a large territory in which to hunt and often roams over 6 miles in a single night. A large reservation has been set aside for the Spanish Lynx's protection.

VICUÑAS live at elevations of 10,000 feet or higher in the Andes of Peru, Chile, and Argentina. As members of the camel family, they are closely related to Guanacos and to the domesticated llamas and alpacas, which live at lower elevations. The Vicuña has been prized for its wool and meat since the days of the Incas, but the Indians took only a few animals at a time from a herd and then did not return to

148

the same area to hunt for several years. Often they set the animals free after shearing them. There were an estimated 1 to 1.5 million Vicuñas then. But the Spaniards and those who followed them took the Vicuña in massive numbers.

Even so, the population of Vicuñas remained at about 400,000 until 1950, when devastating kills reduced their number to a few thousand. Now they are protected by law, but in the remote areas where they live, enforcing the law is not easy. Vicuñas occupy a habitat that puts them in conflict with people and their livestock. Setting aside protected lands may be the only way to save this species.

Vicuñas

ALPINE IBEXES, or wild goats, once inhabited the Alps in large numbers. Since early times, this goat was hunted for its much prized 3½-foot sickle-shaped horns, its meat, and various other parts of the animal, which were used in folk medicine. As early as 1800 the Alpine Ibex was believed doomed to extinction.

Only a few dozen animals were known to still be alive, and these were all owned by one Italian family. Under this family's careful custodianship, the animals slowly increased their numbers. Large preserves were then established in the mountains to assure the animals of a place to live. Now the number of wild Alpine Ibexes exceeds 10,000, and the danger of their extinction seems to have passed.

The similar Cretan Wild Goat, or *Agrimi,* was once widespread in Asia Minor, but over time herds were reduced to fewer than one hundred animals, which lived in the wild mountain regions of Crete. Efforts were made to protect the goats that remained and to establish herds on other islands, but on the whole the efforts were not successful, due to the wild goats' tendency to mate with domestic goats.

Alpine Ibex

Markhor

MARKHORS, the largest of the wild goats, live in the mountains of southern Asia and Asia Minor. They are threatened because of land settlement and the goats' competition for grazing land with domestic livestock. Markhor males, which can weigh up to 200 pounds, are noted for their large and twisted horns that can measure as much as 3 feet in length. These goats also sport a heavy beard that hangs from their chin down to their chest. Spending their summers high on the rocky slopes, Markhors move to lower, warmer elevations in the winter, usually traveling in small groups. Only about a thousand of these animals are still believed to exist today. Few of the countries where they are found give them the protection they need.

Musk-Oxen

MUSK-OXEN are most abundant today in Canada and on Greenland and nearby islands. Their total population is close to 20,000. Once large herds roamed North America and Asia, but their numbers are now down to a few hundred in North America and zero in Asia. These giant shaggy beasts, often weighing more than 900 pounds, do not fare well in captivity. But efforts are being made to return some to the wilds of their native lands—even to Asia. It is hoped that they will make a successful comeback.

Musk-Oxen feed on the mosses, lichens, and low-growing plants of the tundra. In winter they push aside the snow to uncover these plants. Typically they travel in herds of ten or more animals, their numbers giving them protection from wolves and also from the snow and cold winds. If a herd is threatened by an attacker, the cows and calves get in the center of a ring formed by the bulls. The bulls lower their heads to guard the center.

YAKS are huge wild cattle that live at altitudes of up to 20,000 feet on the Tibetan plateau. Their thick shaggy coats make it possible for them to endure the extremely cold weather. The males, or bulls, can weigh as much as a ton; their large, curved horns may measure as long as 3 feet. Although wild Yaks are now endangered, many Yaks have been domesticated.

Yak

153

APPENDIX

HELPFUL ORGANIZATIONS

All state governments and the federal government, in addition to numerous private organizations, are concerned about vanishing species. Government agencies can provide lists of the plants and animals that are under greatest threat. Below are a few of the most prominent and active organizations that offer information as well as opportunities for those who want to get involved.

Fund for Animals, Inc.
200 West 57th Street
New York, NY 10019

International Council for
Bird Preservation
219c Huntingdon Road
Cambridge CB3 0DL
England, U.K.
or 871 Dolly Madison Boulevard
McLean, VA 22101

International Fund for
Animal Welfare
P.O. Box 193
Yarmouth Port, MA 02675

International Union for Conservation of
Nature and Natural Resources (IUCN)
Avenue du Mont-Blanc
CH 1196
Gland, Switzerland

National Audubon Society
950 Third Avenue
New York, NY 10022

National Resources Defense Council
122 East 42nd Street
New York, NY 10168

National Wildlife Federation
1412 16th Street NW
Washington, DC 20036

The Nature Conservancy
1815 North Lynn Street
Arlington, VA 22209

Sierra Club
530 Bush Street
San Francisco, CA 94108

Smithsonian Institution
1000 Jefferson Drive SW
Washington, DC 20560

Wildlife Preservation Trust
International, Inc.
34th Street and Girard Avenue
Philadelphia, PA 19104

The Wildlife Society
5410 Grosvenor Lane
Bethesda, MD 20814

World Wildlife Fund—U.S.
1250 24th Street NW
Washington, DC 20077-7787

PUBLICATIONS

Endangered species make the news with frequency nowadays. Often they are not "good news" stories, but the tide may be turning. Watch for these stories. Also, check out the books listed below and magazines and journals that focus on these issues for the most up-to-date information.

Amos, Enos S., and Roger L. DiSilvestro. *Audubon Wildlife Report.* New York: National Audubon Society, 1985 to present (issued annually).

Burton, John A. (editor). *The Atlas of Endangered Species.* New York: Macmillan Publishing Company, 1991.

Caras, Roger A. *Last Chance on Earth.* New York: Scribner Books, 1972.

Cox, James A. *The Endangered Ones.* New York: Crown Publications, Inc., 1975.

DiSilvestro, Roger L. *The Endangered Kingdom.* New York: John Wiley and Sons, Inc., 1989.

————————. *Audubon Perspectives: Fight for Survival.* New York: John Wiley and Sons, Inc., 1990.

Matthews, John R., and Charles J. Mosely (eds). *The Official World Wildlife Fund Guide to Endangered Species of North America.* Washington, D.C.: Beacham Publishing, Inc., 1990.

Red List of Threatened Animals. IUCN or World Wildlife Fund. Lists some 5,000 species. Updated and added to regularly.

Regenstein, Lewis. *The Politics of Extinction.* New York: Macmillan Publishing Company, 1975.

Steger, Will, and Jon Bowermaster. *Saving the Earth.* New York: Alfred A. Knopf, 1990.

Stonehouse, Bernard. *Saving the Animals.* New York: Macmillan Publishing Company, 1981.

ENDANGERED ANIMALS LIST: COMMON AND SCIENTIFIC NAMES

The scientific names of most animal species discussed in this book are shown here in *italics*. In **heavy type** preceding the "common" name is the text page reference.

47 Addax (*Addax nasomaculatus*)
40 African Elephant (*Loxodonta africana*)
48 African Wild Ass (*Equus asinus*)
29 African Wild Dog (*Lycaon pictus*)

90 American Alligator (*Alligator mississippiensis*)
150 Alpine Ibex (*Capra ibex*)
38 American Bison (*Bison bison*)
146 Andean Cat (*Felis jacobita*)

48 Arabian Oryx (*Oryx leucoryx*)
40 Asian Elephant (*Elephas maximus*)
33 Asiatic Lion (*Panthera leo*)
130 Aye-aye (*Daubentonia madagascariensis*)
95 Bachman's Warbler (*Vermivora bachmanii*)
61 Bald Eagle (*Haliaeetus leucocephalus*)
30 Barbary Hyena (*Hyaena barbara*)
134 Black Ape (*Macaca nigra*)
28 Black-footed Ferret (*Mustela nigripes*)
26 Black-tailed Prairie Dog (*Cynomys ludovicianus*)
108 Blue Whale (*Balaenoptera musculus*)
48 Bontebok (*Damaliscus dorcas*)
76 Brazilian Tapir (*Tapirus terrestris*)
30 Brown Hyena (*Hyaena brunnea*)
103 Brown Pelican (*Pelecanus occidentalis*)
120 Cahow (*Pterodroma cahow*)
139 California Condor (*Gymnogyps californianus*)
95 Cape Sable Sparrow (*Ammospiza mirabilis*)
58 Carolina Parakeet (*Conuropsis carolinensis*)
32 Cheetah (*Acinonyx jubatus*)
141 Chinchilla (*Chinchillula sahamae*)
75 Clouded Leopard (*Neofelis nebulosa*)
81 Colobus Monkey (*Colobus guereza*)
107 Common Dolphin (*Delphinus delphis*)
92 Common Egret (*Casmerodius albus*)
113 Coucal (*Coua delalandei*)
113 Dodo (*Raphus cucullatus*)
76 Duiker (*Cephalophus*)
24 Eastern Gray Kangaroo (*Macropus giganteus*)
114 Elephant Bird (*Aepyornis maximus*)
20 Emu (*Dromaius novaehollandiae*)
94 Eskimo Curlew (*Numenius borealis*)
133 Fat-tailed Dwarf Lemur (*Cheirogaleus medius*)
133 Fork-marked Mouse Lemur (*Phaner furcifer*)

118 Galàpagos Tortoise (*Testudovicina*)
89 Gavial (*Gavialis gangeticus*)
146 Geoffroy's Cat (*Felis geoffroyi*)
97 Giant Otter (*Pteronura brasiliensis*)
146 Giant Panda (*Ailuropoda melanoleuca*)
35 Giant Sable Antelope (*Hippotragus equinus*)
82 Gorilla (*Gorilla gorilla*)
68 Gray Bat (*Myotis grisescens*)
133 Gray Gentle Lemur (*Hapalemur griseus*)
100 Great Auk (*Pinguinus impennis*)
22 Greater Prairie Chicken (*Tympanuchus cupido*)
102 Green turtle (*Chelonia mydas*)
11 Grevy's Zebra (*Equus grevyi*)
144 Grizzly Bear (*Ursus arctos horribilis*)
102 Hawksbill Turtle (*Eretmochelys imbricata*)
58 Heath Hen (*Tympanuchus cupido cupido*)
131 Indri (*Indri indri*)
59 Ivory-billed Woodpecker (*Campephilus principalis*)
71 Jaguar (*Panthera onca*)
126 Jamaican Hutia (*Geocapromys brownii*)
124 Kagu (*Rhynochetos jubatus*)
127 Javan Rhinoceros (*Rhinoceros sondaicus*)
64 Kakapo (*Strigops habroptilus*)
128 Key Deer (*Odocoileus virginianus clavium*)
46 Kit Fox (*Vulpes macrotis*)
65 Kirtland's Warbler (*Dendroica kirtlandii*)
120 Kiwi (*Apteryx australis*)
146 Kodkod (*Felis guigna*)
66 Koala (*Phascolarctos cinereus*)
117 Komodo Dragon (*Varanus komodensis*)
101 Labrador Duck (*Camptorhynchus labradorius*)
80 Langur (*Pygathrix nemaeus*)
74 Leopard (*Panthera pardus*)
88 Leopard Frog (*Rana pipiens*)
22 Lesser Prairie Chicken (*Tympanuchus pallidicinctus*)
33 Lion (*Panthera Leo*)
128 Lowland Anoa (*Anoa depressicornis*)
114 Mamo (Hawaiian Honeycreeper) (*Drepanis pacifica*)

30 Maned Wolf (*Chrysocyon brachyurus*)
75 Margay (*Felis wiedii*)
151 Markhor (*Capra falconeri*)
115 Mauritius Kestrel (*Falco punctatus*)
115 Moa (*Megalopteryx didinus*)
133 Mongoose Lemur (*Lemur mongoz*)
123 Monkey-eating Eagle (*Pithecophaga jefferyi*)
26 Morro Bay Kangaroo Rat (*Dipodomys heermanni morroensis*)
152 Musk-Oxen (*Ovibos moschatus*)
122 Nene (*Branta sandvicensis*)
66 Numbat (*Myrmecobius fasciatus*)
75 Ocelot (*Felis pardalis*)
76 Okapi (*Okapia johnstoni*)
134 Orangutan (*Pongo pygmaeus*)
20 Ostrich (*Struthio camelus*)
34 Pampas Deer (*Ozotoceros bezoarticus*)
30 Pampas Fox (*Dusicyon culpaeus*)
60 Passenger Pigeon (*Ectopistes migratorius*)
78 Père David's Deer (*Elaphurus davidianus*)
13 Peregrine Falcon (*Falco peregrinus*)
28 Pink Fairy Armadillo (*Chlamyphorus truncatus*)
94 Piping Plover (*Charadrius melodus*)
96 Platypus (*Ornithorhynchus anatinus*)
142 Polar Bear (*Thalarctos maritimus*)
107 Porpoise (*Phocoena phocoena*)
36 Pronghorn (*Antilocapra americana*)
34 Przewalski's Horse (*Equus prezwalskii*)
73 Puma (*Felis concolor*)
78 Pygmy Hippopotamus (*Choeropsis liberiensis*)
19 Quagga (*Equus quagga*)
63 Red-billed Curassow (*Crax blumenbachii*)
59 Red-cockaded Woodpecker (*Dendrocopos borealis*)
24 Red Kangaroo (*Megaleia rufa*)
70 Red Wolf (*Canis rufus*)
20 Rhea (*Pterocnemia*)
84 Rhesus Monkey (*Macaca mulatta*)

48 Scimitar-horned Oryx (*Oryx dammah*)
101 Sea Mink (*Mustela vison macrodon*)
104 Sea Otter (*Enhydra lutris*)
24 Short-nosed Rat Kangaroo (*Bettongia lesueur*)
104 Short-tailed (or Steller's) Albatross (*Diomedea albatrus*)
133 Sifaka (*Propithecus*)
92 Snail Kite (*Rostrhamus sociabilis*)
74 Snow Leopard (*Panthera uncia*)
92 Snowy Egret (*Leucophoyx thula*)
126 Solenodon (*Solenodon paradoxus*)
106 Southern Fur Seal (*Arctocephalus townsendi*)
148 Spanish Lynx (*Felis lynx pardina*)
142 Spectacled Bear (*Tremarctos ornatus*)
138 Spectacled Cormorant (*Phalacrocorax perspicillatus*)
62 Spotted Owl (*Strix occidentalis*)
138 Steller's Sea Cow (*Hydrodamalis gigas*)
127 Sumatran Rhinoceros (*Dicerorhinus sumatrensis*)
124 Takahe (*Notornis mantelli*)
129 Tamaraw (*Bubalus mindorensis*)
80 Emperor Tamarin (*Saguinus imperator*)
125 Tasmanian Devil (*Sarcophilus harrisii*)
125 Tasmanian Wolf (*Thylacinus cynocephalus*)
66 Three-toed Sloth (*Bradypus*)
72 Tiger (*Panthera tigris*)
62 Variegated Tinamou (*Crypturellus variegatus*)
116 Tuatara (*Sphenodon punctatus*)
83 Uakari (*Cacajao rubicundus*)
141 Volcano Rabbit (*Romerolagus diazi*)
148 Vicuña (*Vicugna vicugna*)
111 West Indian Manatee (*Trichechus manatus*)
24 Western Hare Wallaby (*Lagorchestes hirsutus*)
36 White-tailed Gnu (*Connochaetes gnou*)
22 Whooping Crane (*Grus americana*)
82 Woolly Spider Monkey (*Brachyteles arachnoides*)
153 Yak (*Bos grunniens*)

INDEX

Italicized page numbers refer to illustrations.